SERIAL AGENCIES

"Frank Kelleter's *Serial Agencies* is a model of the kind of work we dream about but so rarely see in the study of popular serialities—a book that eschews both the easy and threadbare options of by-the-numbers ideological critique and digital age utopianism that imagines unfettered possibilities for readerly agency and empowerment. Kelleter offers a critique of *The Wire* and its cult that is witty, nuanced, and utterly compelling—from his account of how the text produces the conditions of its own reading as the 'greatest show in the history of television,' to his account of the show's nostalgia for models of labor lost in the post-industrial and digital age. Kelleter's analysis extends beyond the show's producers and creators to include the growing army of reviewers, bloggers, and academic critics who all play a role in its circulation. For TV Studies, there is a cautionary tale here very much worth pausing over, wherein the academic celebration of a program confers cultural value with institutional benefits not only to the program's producers but also to the scholars who underwrite the fantasy that 'it's not TV, it's HBO.' It is very much TV, Kelleter reminds us, but a 21st-century TV that expertly manages the post-industrial economies of capital, culture, and citizenship."

Jared Gardner (Ohio State University), author of *Projections: Comics and the History of Twenty-First-Century Storytelling* (Stanford UP, 2011)

"Frank Kelleter's *Serial Agencies* is sharp, savvy, and sophisticated, offering a fresh angle of vision on a much-discussed TV drama. This is a must-read book for fans of *The Wire* as well as

anyone interested in the relations between actor-network-theory and media studies."
Rita Felski (University of Virginia), author of *Uses of Literature* (Wiley-Blackwell, 2008) and editor of *New Literary History*

"Kelleter succeeds in letting us hear what *The Wire* says about itself, what its readers do in their reading practices, and how scholarship shapes its critical objects of serialized culture. In doing so, this engaging book does more than just illuminate this canonical television text; it provides an original approach to understanding serial media and its critical practices. *Serial Agencies* will hopefully prove to be a powerful actor on the future of media and cultural studies."
Jason Mittell (Middlebury College), author of *Television & American Culture* (Oxford UP, 2009)

"Frank Kelleter's analysis of *The Wire* skillfully interrogates the ways in which this TV show has been authorially promoted, journalistically valued, and industrially described. Relating texts to paratexts (whilst cutting across TV Studies and American Studies), Kelleter critically threads together *The Wire*'s pop-cultural circulations, tapping into its serial 'outbidding' and placing its claims to realistic, novelistic, and mythic resonances under the closest of surveillance. Always vigilant and thoughtful, this smart book tackles how *The Wire* has been used, all in the game of cultural and national status. *Serial Agencies* is essential reading for scholars, fans, and aca-fans alike."
Matt Hills (Aberystwyth University), author of *Fan Cultures* (Routledge, 2002)

Serial Agencies

The Wire and Its Readers

Serial Agencies

The Wire and Its Readers

Frank Kelleter

Winchester, UK
Washington, USA

First published by Zero Books, 2014
Zero Books is an imprint of John Hunt Publishing Ltd., Laurel House, Station Approach,
Alresford, Hants, SO24 9JH, UK
office1@jhpbooks.net
www.johnhuntpublishing.com
www.zero-books.net

For distributor details and how to order please visit the 'Ordering' section on our website.

Text copyright: Frank Kelleter 2013

ISBN: 978 1 78279 540 7

A CIP catalogue record for this book is available from the British Library.

Design: Stuart Davies

Printed and bound by CPI Group (UK) Ltd, Croydon, CR0 4YY

We operate a distinctive and ethical publishing philosophy in all
areas of our business, from our global network of authors to
production and worldwide distribution.

CONTENTS

Acknowledgments

At different stages of its development, this study was supposed to become either a contribution to an essay collection on *The Wire* or a chapter within a larger book on serial storytelling in American popular culture. Scholarship being what it is – openended, dialogic, evolving – that second manifestation might still come about. The first one already did: A shorter version of Chapter Two was published as "*The Wire* and Its Readers" in *The Wire: Race, Class, and Genre*, edited by Liam Kennedy and Stephen Shapiro (Ann Arbor: University of Michigan Press, 2012, pp. 33-70). I wish to thank the editors and the University of Michigan Press, particularly Debra Shafer, for granting permission to republish and revise my contribution to their volume.

More people have played a part in bringing this book about than I can possibly acknowledge. Perhaps it all started many years ago, at some party, when I talked with Fotis Jannidis about the merits and scholarly challenges of serial television since *Seinfeld*. Then came "Popular Seriality" and things got moving: an interdisciplinary Research Unit, based primarily at University of Göttingen (2010-2013) and Freie Universität Berlin (2013-2016), consisting of thirteen sub-projects, funded by the German Research Foundation (DFG). I don't know where to begin expressing my debt and gratitude to this fabulous group and its brilliant members and associates. Particularly important to me have been conversations with Regina Bendix, Shane Denson, Christian Hißnauer, Kaspar Maase, Claudia Stockinger, Stefan Scherer, and especially Ruth Mayer, my fellow Americanist, who has shaped my thinking and writing about seriality – and about our field – in countless ways. *Serial Agencies* also draws substantially on my collaborations with Andreas Jahn-Sudmann and Daniel Stein in two of the Unit's subprojects (on the media logic of American "Quality TV" and on the generic history of superhero comics). I hope they will recognize this book as theirs as much as mine – though I will take credit, as the saying goes, for all mistakes. Besides Andreas and Daniel, the following people within and without the Unit read the manuscript and offered suggestion and critique: Jared Gardner, Christy Hosefelder, Susanne Krugmann, Kathleen Loock, and Alexander Starre. Jason Mittell has been a constant source of information and inspiration – as reader, writer, and friend. Anja Johannsen drank beer and wine with me, discussing with me many of the issues raised in this book, without us always realizing that this was what we were discussing. I would also like to thank the participants of my seminar on theory and method at the Graduate School of North American Studies (John F. Kennedy Institute, Freie Universität Berlin), who helped me clarify some of the methodological points in the following chapters. Finally, a hearty Thank You goes to the people at Zero Books. Your interest and enthusiasm convinced me to go ahead with this publication instead of holding it back for what might remain the fantasy of a more comprehensive work on American serialities.

Berlin, February 2014

Introduction

What is *The Wire* to American culture? What work does it perform? Which actions, which actors, does it set into motion? Which discourses and practices are channeled, challenged, or stabilized by this television series?

Such questions, though hardly esoteric, were rarely asked in early analyses of *The Wire*. Instead, the importance of this text – the importance of its arrival on American screens and the importance of its aesthetic innovations – was taken for granted by most writers. Early commentators on *The Wire* treated questions about the show's cultural work as if they were already answered. Much was certain before the various "studies" set out to do their work of explication, even as the show was still running: *The Wire*, one could read, revolutionizes American television with dense storytelling. It paints an uncompromising image of the institutional, economic, and racial dimensions of inner-city decline. In painstaking detail and epic breadth, it brings to light what the American media have so far kept in the dark. It formulates a sophisticated indictment of post-industrial capitalism. It critiques the state of a nation which thinks it can afford to ignore these harsh realities. In a word, *The Wire* is "the best television show ever."

How did everyone know?

By watching *The Wire*, no doubt. But what does that mean? When Jacob Weisberg, in his influential *Slate* article on September 13, 2006, called *The Wire* "surely the best TV show ever broadcast in America," he (and other commentators making similar assessments at the time) did not, properly speaking, initiate this topos.[1] True, a look at the first published reactions to *The Wire* reveals that journalism and the blogosphere were influential in setting the tone and agenda of many subsequent academic discussions (probably indicating the growing alignment of both spheres, not least in the shrinking time available in either for written reactions).[2] But before any so-called external observer ever offered an interpretation of the series, the series did so itself – and not only in the sense of providing an occasion for exegetic follow-up, simply by being itself, but in the more active sense of producing self-descriptions that have steered its cultural work and activated narrative practices outside its textual boundaries, so that the very identification of narrative and text – i.e., the notion that serial storytelling is contained within a bound and clearly addressable composition – loses some of its analytic plausibility.

In the following chapters, I will discuss (1) the ways in which *The Wire* has been reading itself, (2) the ways in which Anglo-American scholars have been reading *The Wire*, and (3) the ways in which serial self-descriptions and critical practices have been interacting within the larger system of American (popular) culture. I will argue that the show's aesthetics and its academic reception fulfill mutually dependent functions – in fact, that they perform mutually dependent *actions* – within an overarching sphere of national auto-reference. The *Wire* phenomenon, comprising the media text of the series and its public accompaniments, mobilizes practices and values that help stabilize America's conflict-ridden conceptualization of itself.

1

Self-Descriptions

Can a television series watch itself? Can a text read itself? Can a text read anything? Not like an intentional person, for sure, but then the question can be turned around: How many texts, how many readings, are present in a person's intentions and judgments? And is their presence not an active one – one that produces further dealings and motions, without necessarily determining them? Who is acting when a writer "follows" an aesthetic decision she has made? Effective in that decision, as in its consequences, are always other agencies, some far removed from the person acting, some not known to her, some not even human.

I am, of course, advocating a concept of agency as developed and employed in Actor-Network-Theory (ANT), most notably by Bruno Latour, who declares that "objects too have agency."[3] This counterintuitive statement lends itself to critical caricature – or, conversely, to a certain theoretical bravado. But stressing the agency of objects does not mean to make "the empty claim that objects do things 'instead' of human actors." According to Latour, it means "to accept that the continuity of any course of action will rarely consist of human-to-human connections . . . or of object-to-object connections but will probably zigzag from one to the other." As a result, the term "actor" in Actor-Network-Theory simply refers, in Latour's words, to "something which makes us do things." This sounds less exciting than post-anthropocentric epistemologies would have it, but the emphasis on doing makes all the difference. If taken seriously, a practice-centered perspective has far-reaching consequences. To begin with, it invites us to understand the term "network" not simply as a figure of people or places or things intricately connected but as that which makes such connections possible: a dynamic of interlocking actions. On this view, to study culture means to investigate specific (historical) processes of assembling, not just the results of certain assemblages. It means to study structure as consolidated action, to redescribe as mobile what has established itself as settled, to examine networks as work-nets of agency.[4]

So, yes, a text can read itself and describe itself, especially if that text is a serial one – i.e., one that evolves in a feedback loop with its own effects – and if by "text," we mean not something that is but something that does: not a single outlook or structure waiting to be decoded or uncovered but an entanglement of textual practices. If network analysis is interested in specific acts of connection, not just their material outcome, the very specificity of these interactions encourages us to regard networks as empirically real, i.e., as consisting of plausibly traceable actions rather than random or interesting associations that can be established between, say, a television series and some philosophical perspective we happen to subscribe to. With this thought in mind, I propose a methodological model that attempts to combine ANT's micro-perspective with a systems-theoretical macro-perspective (relying chiefly on conceptual tools provided by Niklas Luhmann's version of systems theory).[5] ANT stresses the mobility of actors and the domain-independent openness of their exchanges, while systems theory investigates the emergence of improbable stabilities and the self-generation of unlikely boundaries. Trying to do justice, respectively, to the reality of distinct spheres of social action and the existence of constant traffic between them, both perspectives are compatible when they describe culture as something that keeps *happening* – something that keeps ensuring the continuation of its own existence, enlisting for this purpose different players and products, ambitions and commitments, affiliations and identifications.

But this is better shown than declared. Hence, I will hereafter refrain from addressing the "Theory" part of these critical ensembles, Actor-Network-Theory and systems theory. My aim is neither to show that ANT makes sense to itself nor to refine system theory's scholastic auto-references. My aim is merely to put these descriptive tools to use as sensitizing concepts, hoping to launch an investigation that will be adjusted to the empirical movements of empirical actors. With regard to a television series – inevitably multi-authored, produced and consumed in many-layered systems of responsibility and performance, always dependent on the material demands of its medium and the constraints of its institutional environments – it seems particularly appropriate to think of agency (and certainly authorship) as something dispersed in a network of people, institutions, technologies, objects, and forms. This is why, in the following, I will refer to *The Wire* as an actor-network that comprises both the television narrative of the same title and the communicative practices accompanying the discrete television text. The plausibility of this descriptive move should not depend on its agreement or non-agreement with some Theory but should become obvious when it is performed.[6]

Personal vision and intentional choices are certainly of consequence in serial storytelling, as are copyrights and proper names, but a television series is never authored by any *one* writer, producer, or even company. There are many reasons for this, among them the fact that serial publication by definition overlaps with serial reception. A series, unlike a self-contained oeuvre, can observe its own effects on audiences as long as the narrative is running. Moreover, it can react to these observations, making adjustments in form and content, just as audiences can become active in a narrative's development if the narrative is still unfolding – if it is a serial narrative, that is. The commercial framework of such transactions further complicates established distinctions between production and reception, authors and readers, intentions and objects.[7]

Thus, instead of proceeding from the assumption that *The Wire* is "David Simon's *The Wire*" or "HBO's *The Wire*," we can ask how the show came to be perceived in these ways – and what the practical (i.e., action-bound) consequences of such perceptions are in terms of its evolving relation to itself, to its viewers, and ultimately to the larger cultural system from which it draws and to which it contributes. As befits a work-net of agencies – and as befits a commercial series – *The Wire* is busy describing itself at different levels of public discourse, setting in motion different actors and deploying different textual modes.[8] For one thing, paratextual commentaries by producers (of whatever status), in interviews or on DVD special features, suggest how the series wants to be watched. Moreover, *The Wire* already interprets itself in its narrative and the very act of telling a story. In fact, any popular series is forced to keep creating identities in reaction to understandings and ascriptions brought forth by its continued existence. To the extent that a long run keeps involving ever more actors in the narrative – or keeps enlisting ever more involved actors – the boundaries between text and paratext are in need of constant revision if a series wants to maintain control of its public actions.[9] In the following, I will delineate three identities constructed by *The Wire* for itself: its institutional identity (as an HBO Original Series), its artistic identity (as a specific type of journalistic fiction), and its narrative identity (as a complex serial). Bound up with these constructions are other modes of self-description that I will touch on, concerning genre, casting, character constellation, and social criticism.

Outdoing HBO

In his introduction to a semi-promotional volume called *The Wire: Truth Be Told*, edited by Rafael Alvarez (a writer for the show), David Simon reiterates a point often made in early interviews: *The Wire*, Simon says, "could not exist but for HBO" and its pay-TV model.[10] As an expensive premium channel, financed largely by viewer subscriptions, HBO is not in the business of attracting advertisers. Instead, it addresses viewers directly as consumers of its media products. The most visible effect of this subscription model is that there are no commercials on HBO, except for those that advertise the channel itself. Since the 1990s, this business model (with some variation in other pay channels) has proven innovative for American television in a number of ways. To begin with, it allows for different rhythms of storytelling (there is no need for repeated cliffhangers that try to make audiences stay tuned during commercial breaks). Furthermore, as Simon stresses, the absence of commercials creates an altogether different attitude toward storytelling. In selling stories to audiences rather than selling audiences to advertisers, HBO and other subscription channels are more likely to take risks with unconventional material. According to Simon, they are also more writer-centered in their production policies than the networks.[11] In addition, a pay-TV channel can ignore the concerns of external parties, such as advertisers, who may not want to see their names or products associated with socially divisive content.

Altogether, cable television is less dependent on the broadcasting model of American television. It no longer has to abide by the ideal of television as a "cultural forum," i.e., as a medium that offers a wide array of opinions and perspectives within one and the same program in order to appeal to a broad demographic.[12] On this logic, designing programs for smaller target groups – narrowcasting – pushes the boundaries of what can be shown and told on television.

Of course, the contemporaneous example of opinion journalism produced by and for homogenous political constituencies casts some doubt on the inherent "quality" of niche programming. Perhaps the progressive feel of HBO productions in the 1990s and 2000s has more to do with the economic and social status of the channel's customers than with the channel's freedom from broadcasting ideals. Be that as it may,

HBO is first and foremost a commercial institution, even and especially in its elite appeal (as illustrated by the channel's failure to continue ambitious programs such as *Deadwood* and *Carnivàle*). In this sense, each HBO Original Series, while free of commercial interruptions, is in fact an intricate and expensive commercial for the channel itself. "It's not TV. It's HBO" was the station's much-quoted marketing slogan between 1996 and 2009, summarizing a claim of media-historical innovation staggering in its proportions. The aim has been to establish a supposedly new, supposedly oxymoronic phenomenon and to identify it exclusively with HBO: televisual quality.[13] In David Simon's statement about the beneficial results of HBO's economic model, *The Wire* participates in this identification.

It should be noted that HBO's self-positioning owes much to a principle deeply ingrained in popular seriality: one-upmanship, i.e., the tendency of serial narratives to surpass and outbid each other.[14] As a strategy of competitive continuity, one-upmanship or outbidding (*Überbietung*) comes naturally to commercial series, even when they claim distinction by virtue of artistic quality rather than quantitative accomplishments (a more typical form of one-upmanship). Note, in this context, that the label "Quality TV" itself performs an act of outbidding in the field of commercial production: an act of outbidding that points beyond popular culture and mobilizes the highbrow potentials of serial television. *The Wire*'s insistence on generic innovation, for example, is intimately tied up with the show's attitude toward network competitors. "Swear to God," declares Simon, "it was never a cop show . . . it was never entirely appropriate to classify it as a crime story."[15] He goes on to describe how he pitched the project to HBO:

> The show's emphasis on surveillance would be new, and the tone of the piece was different from network fare, but *The Wire*, as it began to be called, still appeared to be a cop show.

And HBO's primary concern became apparent: if the networks do cop shows, why are we doing one? The nightmare was to imagine critics across the country finally declaring that this was not in fact HBO, but TV.

A number of points are noteworthy about this statement. First, Simon explicitly affirms that aesthetic agency is dispersed within a set of real and imagined, physical and immaterial actors. The show's generic shape was *made*, he says, not by the unilateral intentions of a creator-individual or by the economic interests of an institution, but by a dynamic network which includes genre rules, audience expectations, and even the future actions of absent and hypothetical actors (critics across the country calling it all a sham).

Consequently, and secondly, it becomes clear that one of the most consistently praised qualities of *The Wire* – its originality in terms of genre – does not result from any one "source" (the creator's aesthetic vision, the institution's commercial calculations, the text's social criticism, the producers' or consumers' search for social distinction, etc.) but emerged from often discordant interactions among a variety of players. So while the qualities of Quality TV are inextricably interwoven with economic and institutional concerns, it would be mistaken to think of this insight as one that "uncovers" the true forces at work behind the text's surface actions. Aesthetic qualities, while certainly not operating in an ontological realm of their own, are no delegates of other, hidden purposes, nor are they simply ascribed from an outside world of social interests. Instead, they perform lively work in connecting and disconnecting the text to and from other practices and practitioners.[16]

Thirdly, Simon's reminder that *The Wire* is an HBO Original Series – an identity central to its aesthetic operations – is part of a larger argument which clandestinely brings into play yet another type of authorship for the series: one that, controversially, understands itself as non-institutional and non-commercial. In a 2006 interview, Simon qualifies his praise of HBO with the following, slyly contradictory sentences:

> There were no models for us in TV. I admire the storytelling of *The Sopranos*, though I don't watch it consistently. And *Deadwood*; I don't watch it, but I admire their storytelling. We certainly weren't paying attention to network TV.[17]

The claim of generic originality ("no models for us in TV") is still conjoined here with a gesture of respect for HBO, but Simon's admiration for shows he does not watch also disconnects *The Wire* from the aesthetics of its closest institutional neighbors. The implication is that he and his collaborators were not paying much attention to HBO either. As an HBO Original Series, *The Wire* explores territory that no network series had explored before. But this statement can be topped: As an HBO Original Series among others, *The Wire* is still sui generis. It's not HBO, it's David Simon & Co.

Simon's disclaimer of competitive impulses is belied by its competitive performance – a meandering sense of rivalry mostly directed against *The Sopranos*. Narrative practice shows as much. *The Wire* takes care to distance itself visually, atmospherically, and by other means from *The Sopranos* and *Deadwood*, even as it profits from institutional and artistic associations with these "complex" series. Visually, for example, *The Wire* uses a traditional 4:3 aspect ratio through all five seasons, relinquishing the more cinematic 16:9 aspect ratio so effectively put to use by other HBO shows. As a result, the series actually looks more like conventional TV than most quality productions of the time. In this context, it is worth mentioning that *The Wire* apparently started as a project about crime in 1960s Baltimore, to be told as a tragedy that would wed the tone of Shakespeare's history plays to the style of classic gangster movies. (As reporter for the

Baltimore Sun, Simon once wrote "an extended comparison of a convicted drug dealer and Shakespeare's Richard III.")[18] We might speculate if Simon's abandonment of this project in favor of a more sociological approach to urban crime had something to do with the conspicuous deployment of tragic modes in *The Sopranos* and Shakespearean language in *Deadwood*. Still, Simon is unwilling to surrender the term "tragedy" completely. Pointing to a difference between Greek and Shakespearean tragedy, he associates *The Wire* with the former:

> I enjoy Shakespeare but *The Wire* is definitely not influenced by the good-evil continuum that seems to begin with Shakespearean drama. It's more about fate and systematic predestination, with the Olympian gods supplanted by postmodern institutional authority.[19]

In the same interview, Simon situates HBO's *The Sopranos* alongside popular network series such as *24* and *Desperate Housewives* to argue that the successes of these programs originate in their "whiteness," whereas *The Wire* is simply "too black" to achieve comparable ratings. Concerning their aesthetic consequences, both descriptions are related to each other: If the tragic model of *The Wire* is different from the tragic model of Shakespeare (as understood by Simon) and if the series hearkens back to the older heritage of Greek drama, updating it for postmodern times, this marks *The Wire* as a program that does not exactly compete with other prestigious productions, including HBO's own, but transcends the commercial bounds of Quality TV altogether. To underline this point, Simon suggests that the show's non-institutional identity is clearly evidenced by its economically counter-intuitive decision to tell a story largely centered on the black underclass of a city as unglamorous as Baltimore.

This may well be the most powerful, certainly the most influential description *The Wire* has produced about itself: that it is a racial minority drama in which the city of Baltimore is rendered so authentically that it becomes a virtual character in the narrative. I will disregard for a moment the racial dimension of this statement and concentrate on *The Wire*'s self-understanding as a show not so much *about* but *of* Baltimore. Despite Simon's repeated claims that *The Wire* represents, on a more abstract level, the post-industrial city worldwide, the series works hard at various levels to make us understand it could not be set in any other place – that Baltimore is, in effect, not simply its setting but its home. The casting of locals, the employment of insider anecdotes later explained in the national press, on-location shooting, cameos, and especially the much-publicized biographical involvement of David Simon – these actions serve to produce an all-important effect: this is real.[20]

Three points on *The Wire* as a narrative of Baltimore. First, choosing a counter-intuitive setting is actually in accordance with HBO's established policies of distinction. Such choice can even be regarded as another act of one-upmanship, i.e., as the series' attempt to gain competitive edge through a location even more unlikely than others. In a similar way, *The Sopranos* successfully distinguished itself from cinematic predecessors by setting its gangster epic exactly not in New York, but across the river in the suburbs of New Jersey.[21]

Secondly, setting the show in Baltimore is not "just" (or "really") a competitive choice. The same act that can advance HBO's position as an elite channel, "going where no network could compete" (Simon), can serve Simon's own attempt to distance himself from HBO's commercial interests.[22] In this sense, the choice of Baltimore has direct consequences for the way urban space is represented in and by the series, namely as a specific scene, not mere scenery. In turn, making Baltimore become active in the narrative advances the show's key effect of authenticity. When Simon cites his double status as a long-time

Baltimorean and television outsider to underline that *The Wire* is a show about minorities made by minorities (of sorts), this is not just a cover-up for the accumulation of counter-cultural capital. As Jason Mittell reminds us, the show's staff is indeed full of people who never wrote or acted for television before.[23]

Thus, the claim that this is "not TV" is not entirely wrong; many people working on the series are really from Baltimore and many are really television outsiders. But what does that mean? Again I suggest that we approach *The Wire*'s claim of maverick authenticity – as well as the show's performance of maverick authenticity – not as a matter of fact nor as a false pretense that hides other motives, but as an action in tie with other actions: Just as the conspicuous display of local knowledge by Simon and other personnel lends credibility to the show's aesthetic operations, so the show's credibility and aesthetic give incentive and guidance to the ways Simon and others can present and understand themselves as Baltimoreans (in public, on blogs, perhaps even privately). This circuit of actions is not restricted to industrial producers; it continues, as Chapter Two will show, in public and academic responses to *The Wire*, where the local credentials of those who speak – i.e., the questions: where are you from? what do you know? what have you seen? etc. – gain significance and channel further doings.

Thirdly, Simon's wish to distance himself from other HBO competitors felicitously feeds back into HBO's business model. In fact, this feedback plays a decisive part in the show's sustained success – a success that cannot be measured in ratings or Emmys won, but might well depend on the fact, often emphasized, that the show won no Emmys and had remarkably low ratings.[24] (Things might look different for DVD sales.) In the subscription model of television, prestige can translate directly into money. This helps explain why HBO in the late 1990s and early 2000s attracted so many charismatic and headstrong creator-types: people like David Simon, David Chase, or David Milch, whose self-understanding mirrors the habitus of strong authors in the field of canonized production, who for the longest time have described themselves as unmindful of, even averse to, commercial motives. Such risky personalities are profitable – to a degree – for an enterprise bent on producing "not TV" because they can bring the ambitions and performances of authorized art to multi-authored mass productions.

But the crucial term is "can." The limits of this business model are easily visible; its success depends on fortuitous constellations, such as the unexpected, self-reinforcing triumph of *The Sopranos*. As mentioned above, already *Deadwood* and especially *Carnivàle* stretched HBO's artistic ambitions beyond the point of financial feasibility. True, in the history of American television formal innovations have often involved strong creator figures (Bill Cosby, Joss Whedon, etc.), but under the network system, creatorship has commonly been framed as an (oppositional) exception to the (standardized) rule. HBO may be the first channel that profited – at least for a while – from a production policy that put individual vision center stage in the supply-and-demand economy of serial television. The story with which this new authorship-type likes to describe and celebrate itself was recently canonized in Brett Martin's popular book *Difficult Men* (2013): Television's true artists, Martin claims, are just as tough and nonconformist as the (male) characters with which they revolutionized the medium.

Supplanting the Novel

"We are misfits," David Simon told Nick Hornby about the makers of *The Wire*, "none of us think of ourselves as providing entertainment. The impulse is . . . either journalistic or literary."[25] Among all self-descriptions of *The Wire*, its identity as a crypto-literary work, a "televised novel," was among the first to be picked up and developed by commentators and critics. Jacob Weisberg based his statement about "the best TV show ever broadcast" somewhat illogically "not . . . on my having seen all the possible rivals for the title but on the premise that no other program has ever done anything remotely like what this one does, namely to portray the social, political, and economic life of an American city with the scope, observational precision, and moral vision of great literature." Weisberg's "premise" is exactly that: a hypothesis that would require having seen possible rivals to be able to even make the statement it makes. As it stands, the content of Weinberg's proposal (*The Wire* does what great literature does) is carried over from *The Wire*'s own public demeanor.[26]

On closer inspection, the show enacts its literary identity in a manner more ambivalent than suggested by the widespread talk of its novelistic qualities. A number of artistic associations can be distinguished, and they do not always harmonize, offering analysts opportunities to put forth competing readings and classifications. I already mentioned *The Wire*'s competitive self-definition as a narrative in the tradition of Greek rather than Shakespearean drama. Already in its first versions (by Simon), this reading was usually expanded to stress the show's systemic approach, i.e., its contemporary interest in institutional structures (formerly: fate) rather than characters.

Even more frequently, *The Wire* provokes associations with the 19th-century social novel. Charles Dickens is quoted persistently, and journalistic as well as internet discussions have consolidated this connection into a topos. Subsequently, it has migrated with some refinements and qualifications into academic discourse, where its presence can be felt whenever the show's realism is lauded or taken for granted. A notable exception can be found in the field of TV studies, where some scholars have pointed to the self-serving nature of *The Wire*'s courtship of Dickensian or generally novelistic affiliations. Perceiving such comparisons as marketing ploys, press inventions, or strategies intent on cultural prestige, these scholars stress *The Wire*'s artistic identity as a television series. To treat the show like a novel, they argue, denigrates the qualities of its medium – a complaint that, in turn, expresses concern about the prestige of their own field and practice.[27]

Certainly *The Wire*'s existence as a commercial series is crucial to its cultural work, as will be discussed in the next chapter. At this point, I focus on the novelistic nexus: What does it mean to say that *The Wire* is "like a novel"? How is this relationship executed? What effects are coming to pass? Which conflicts are present in this statement of connection?

It turns out that the Dickensian comparison rampant in newspapers and on the web is a somewhat diminished version of the show's self-presentation as a fictional narrative. As Simon told *The Guardian*: "It's fiction, I'm clear about that. But at its heart it's journalistic."[28] What reads like a mere conjunction (novel plus journalism) on closer inspection reveals an intricate literary project with a respectable pedigree. Simon has a particular type of novel in mind when he asserts that *The Wire* behaves like one. More importantly, he refers to a particular type of journalism when he calls his show journalistic at heart – a type of journalism that carries with it a clear-cut understanding of the *relationship* between fictional and factual representation. Repeated references to "the way we live now" give it away: *The Wire* heavily draws on the New Journalism of the 1960s and 1970s, defined by Tom Wolfe as a kind of para-factual writing that brings together the virtues of reportage – "legwork, 'digging,' in order to *get it just right*" – with the immersive techniques of 19th-century realist storytelling.[29]

Tom Wolfe's desire to elevate modern non-fiction to the rhetorical standards of Dickens and Balzac was deeply compet-itive. According to Wolfe, to make reportages read *like* novels required "more than mere emulation"; if successful, this aesthetic move would "wipe out the novel as literature's main event." The aim was not to produce better fiction in the guise of journalism, but to "seize the power" of fiction in order to capture reality even more effectively. Historically, Wolfe explained, there had always been an "obvious relationship between reporting and the major novels." Now the time had come to put this relationship from its head onto its feet.[30]

Apparently, David Simon considers himself a worker in the same movement. His commitment to a reportorial concept of reality is beyond doubt and it guides *The Wire*'s relationship to its own fictionality in important ways. As a former reporter for the *Baltimore Sun* and author of two non-fiction novels – that pet genre of the 1970s – Simon plays a role for *The Wire* that exceeds the influence of even the strongest type of television creator or showrunner, exactly because his biography and personality are major forces in the series' performance of itself, lending credibility to a text whose narrative effects are fundamentally premised on appearing credible without requiring suspension of disbelief.[31]

Thus, the show's literary identity – particularly its attitude toward the novel – is as ambiguous as its identity as an HBO Original Series. On the one hand, *The Wire* pays explicit tribute to its novelistic forebears and profits from their prestige and activities. The model in question is not so much the social realism of Dickens and Balzac – notwithstanding public declarations to the contrary – but literary naturalism of the late 19th and early 20th centuries.[32] Many ruling assumptions of the series, such as its appreciation of scope and precision in representation, its fascination with the lower classes, and above all its belief in the priority of environment over character, derive from (American) naturalism's philosophical investment in scientism, anti-gentility, and determinism.

On the other hand, *The Wire* confronts the naturalistic novel as a contestant, trying not only to live up to its example but to supplant it. Marked differences abound. For example, *The Wire* explicitly renounces naturalism's non-judgmental stance. Simon wears his convictions on his sleeve and so does *The Wire*. Often, this makes the series resemble, in Simon's words, "an editorial . . . an angry op-ed."[33] As Linda Williams has shown, this interpretation of the show fails to account for its narrative power, which is based to a large extent on providing multiple character perspectives.[34] But implicit in Simon's assessment is a conflict between factuality and fictionality itself, which in Simon's influential take on the show is always resolved in favor of reportage. According to this prominent self-description of the series – and in a gesture that has become widespread in many sociological usages of *The Wire* as well – the narrative's fictional status is explicitly conceded ("of course it's fiction") only to be subtracted again from the show's cultural operations as a strategic matter of form: Simon has gone on the record saying that the story could not have been broadcast as a documentary exactly *because* it is so accurate. The story had no choice but to resort to fiction to make its point.[35]

In this manner, one of *The Wire*'s most powerful actors declares the show's fictional dealings to be subservient to its factual interests. Such an attitude is bound to have consequences for the narrative. For instance, the show's visual reserve – which made Mittell remark that in terms of style, *The Wire* "appears more akin to conventional procedurals like *Law & Order* than contemporary innovators like *The Sopranos* or *24*" – is entirely attuned to its belief in the transparency of social reality.[36] *The Wire* is deeply confident that privileged access and sustained attention guarantees accuracy of coverage. This is a reporter's confidence. As Tom Wolfe put it, it is "all important to *be there*."[37] The reporter's presence at places closed to public observation opens them up to representation; his or her account is the trustworthy displacement of the public's uninformed distance. As I will discuss in Chapter Three, this ethos of reportage strongly tends to identify (national) reality with what is hidden away from view: a potentially paranoid notion of authenticity.

Moreover, the aspiration to capture unfamiliar life by sheer force of local knowledge contains a didactic attitude. Tom Wolfe said he wanted "to show the reader *real life* – 'Come here! Look! This is the way people live these days! These are the things they do!'" *The Wire* chimes in. One of the show's ambitions seems to be that future researchers trying to learn something about urban America in the early 21st century will turn, not to novels or histories, but to *The Wire* as the text that best portrays the post-industrial city. Despite all its inside jokes, the series counts on an ideal viewer who is (yet) uninformed about its subject matter.[38] At the same time, its will to instruction differs from Wolfe's reportages about the lives of the rich, beautiful, and weird. Unlike such bohemian missives, *The Wire* tells a powerful tale of downward identification, as I will argue. What Linda Williams has identified as Simon's "ethnographic imaginary"[39] – long-term documentary attention resulting in long-term (melo)dramatic storytelling – offers viewers the gratification of feeling like insiders to hidden reality themselves: to join the few who have seen the show, or seen it first, or shared its knowledge, or shared it most knowingly. As we will see in Chapter Two, the fictions of *The Wire* have been accepted as accurate accounts not only by those whose only knowledge of Baltimore derives from *The Wire* but also by teachers (and possibly students) of sociology from Harvard to Leeds.

It would be easy to dismiss such short-cuts as misreadings but they ratify an opinion the show holds about itself. If fiction serves factual reportage, *The Wire*'s conspicuous aversion to the idea of inventing things is no coincidence. When, in the fifth season, the hierarchy of fact and fiction is finally inverted, as if by way of experiment, the results are perverse representations. A bad reporter, Templeton, makes up imaginary informants and a serial killer to advance his career. Significantly, *The Wire* associates this wickedness with realist *fiction*: The man is in search of "the whole Dickensian aspect" when he spends a night

Serial Agencies

with the homeless to get the feel of the street. "The Dickensian Aspect" is the title of episode 5.6; the newspaper's executive editor, Whiting, tells Templeton that this is what he expects from him. Note how this episode mirrors Tom Wolfe's disgust for "human interest stories," which he describes as "long and often hideously sentimental accounts of hitherto unknown souls beset by tragedy or unusual hobbies."[40]

Templeton's journalism is like *The Wire*'s own dark double. Accordingly fierce is the show's indictment of him, one of its few truly despicable characters. Conversely, *The Wire*'s own acts of making-up are in constant need of textual and paratextual safety valves which proclaim the truthful foundation of fictional representation. An impressive array of real-life models are mustered, on which the characters, localities, and plots of the series are said to be based. It is as if the power of this narrative resides not in its telling – this is not the power of fiction! – but, as Wolfe claimed of his own writing, in "the simple fact that the reader knows *all this actually happened*." Incessantly, almost nervously, *The Wire* provides this proof, within and without its narrative: provisions that have traveled into public and academic communications, where they have generated such oxymoronic notions as the "true anecdote" and "authentic fiction."[41]

It is risky business for fiction to denounce itself. Indeed, when Simon's personal involvement began to eclipse other narrative concerns, the fortunate interlocking of authorial and textual doings reached its breaking point. In terms of autobiographical veracity, Season Five should actually have been the most credible. Centered largely on the role played by the struggling *Baltimore Sun* in the city's life of crime and politics, this season, one might think, would supply the most reliable account among its social studies. Instead, it supplied the most reliable account of David Simon's judgments and prejudices. The fifth season introduced a saintly old-school reporter – Gus Haynes, an obvious stand-in for Simon – who is beset by managerial newspaper executives and

20

ambitious young cheats modeled on Simon's ex-colleagues at the *Sun*. It is hard not to read these episodes as a personal feud.

Interestingly, such score-settling provoked the first truly critical reactions to *The Wire* – and their critique was directed at Simon's private investment in the story. In the January/February 2008 issue of *The Atlantic*, Mark Bowden suggested that Simon's "anger about capitalism and the devaluation of human life is rooted in his unhappy existence at *The Sun*." Thus, Bowden found the show's credibility compromised by authorial grudges – and with it, *The Wire*'s entire journalistic habitus:

> He has created his own Baltimore. . . . "*Wire*-world," as Simon calls it, does for turn-of-the-millennium Baltimore what Dickens's *Bleak House* does for mid-19th-century London. . . . [But] like Dickens's London, Simon's Baltimore is a richly imagined caricature of its real-life counterpart. . . . And precisely because the Baltimore in *The Wire* seems so real, down to the finest details, the show constitutes an interesting study in the difference between journalism and fiction.[42]

It is curious that Bowden's suggestions – fairly standard analytical fare (think Barthes's reality effect) – have so far failed to inspire sustained investigation into the narrative strategies of *The Wire*. Instead, Bowden's essay has mostly been used for challenging the show's activist utility and, of course, served as a target for Simon's scattered ripostes. I shall return to this question. At this point, suffice it to say that the fifth season marks no dramatic departure from the series' appreciation of local knowledge and first-hand involvement – which made at least two commentators wonder if the "oversimplifications" of this season, with its pervasive *Lou Grant* air, did not bring to attention "the oversimplifications of seasons past."[43] Most critics, however, detected apostasy and attributed it to Simon. It was as if the author had betrayed his own vision, or rather: the demands of his creation. What better evidence for the agency of aesthetic forms than the possibility of quoting a text against its author? The requirements of a given medium, the necessities that come with the establishment of a style, the implications of a chosen approach: Once a path is taken, it is also this path, and not the traveler alone, that makes the wandering.

Complicating the Series

If reporting an unknown reality is one of *The Wire*'s key ambitions, complexity of narrative structure is another. At its most simple, this characterizes the show as difficult to watch. Producers and critics alike have stressed the series' *demanding* nature, associating it with types of reception usually reserved for works of art: "The first thing we had to do," Simon explains, "was to teach folks to watch television in a different way, to slow themselves down and pay attention, to immerse themselves in a way that the medium had long ago ceased to demand."[44]

Such difficulty serves to distinguish *The Wire* from network entertainment, but it can also be used as an increasable asset on the competitive field of quality productions. In fact, most contrastive references are to other HBO series, especially *The Sopranos*. For example, statements about the show's scope are almost always framed in the rhetoric of competitive comparison so typical of inter-serial outbidding: *The Wire*, we are told, has more plots and characters (and more swear words) than other ambitious series of the time. Scholarly descriptions, too, abound with comparatives and superlatives.[45]

Size obviously matters in the current understanding of what constitutes the qualities of Quality TV. Metaphors of vastness and expansiveness play a conspicuous role in contemporary television criticism, not only with regard to *The Wire*. Ever wider story arcs or ever more, and more entangled, story lines are regularly cited as hallmarks of complexity, and hence of heightened quality *in comparison with* earlier seasons or other series.[46] Simultaneously, the same rhetoric has taught us to speak of television series as singular works of art. The tension between both positions has received little critical attention so far, but it indicates that scholarship on Quality TV is more deeply involved in the serial activities of its material than is suggested by the standard philological distinction between text and criticism.

At the same time, complexity for *The Wire* means more than difficulty. To begin with, the textual demands of the series – such as its renunciation of recaps or its rejection of flashbacks – are closely related to its para-journalistic self-image. If "the show's point of view" is "that of the insider," as Simon stresses, it makes sense that there is "no intention of impairing that point of view by pausing to catch up the audience."[47] In turn, the narrative's refusal to explain everything invites viewers to identify with its performance of privileged knowledge.

Furthermore, *The Wire* is obviously *about* complexity. Unlike other contemporary dramas of entanglement, most notably the network series *Lost*, which implements a puzzle structure that piles, campaign-like, mystery on mystery, the ambition of *The Wire* is not to present sensational solutions to cascading riddles. Instead, and true to its journalistic ethos and its kinship with "multisited ethnography," *The Wire* attempts to show a social system at work: to "build a whole city."[48] True to its naturalistic commitments, too, it attempts to show individuals determined by institutions and their rules. And true to its artistic aspirations – reference points are self-contained modes such as classical drama and the novel – it opts for a systematic and well-ordered approach to render visible the maze of urban institutions: Each season focuses on another Baltimore institution (law enforcement and the drug trade in Season One, labor in Season Two, politics in Season Three, education in Season Four, the news media in Season Five). It is an almost Luhmannesque panorama of "social systems."

In terms of the show's narrative identity, this systematic – and systemic – approach inevitably complicates *The Wire*'s attitude toward its own seriality. Consider that a series, no matter if it is told in episodic or ongoing continuations, differs from a closed work in a number of ways. I have already pointed to the increase of self-observation in serial storytelling and the resulting destabilization of textual boundaries. There are narratological differences as well. In serial stories (both on the episodic and the sequential end of the seriality-spectrum), narrative organization commonly takes place on the go. In consequence, these texts are regularly more untidy than work-bound structures.[49] The demands of serial self-innovation are such that the amount of narrative information to be arranged increases with each episode, but usually, because of the underlying commercial production culture, there is no over-arching trajectory toward closure, which would allow the story to systematize its innovations from the perspective of a pre-arranged ending. What is more, there is no possibility to revise the narrative before publication to get rid of inconsistencies. Serial narratives have to do their work of pruning, control, and coordination *within* the narrative. Hence all these ongoing self-descriptions. As a result, series typically abound with false starts and loose ends, especially when read in their entirety.

In this sense, serial storytelling has always unfolded in a sprawl, from the beginning of commercial serialization in the early 19th century to the digital age.[50] When contemporary television series set out to organize this sprawl into narrative "complexity," they are, in fact, working on something that is an inevitable result of commercial serialization anyway. One manner of performing this work in a plausible manner – and establishing plausibility has been an enduring and challenging task for commercial series (think *Dallas* 9.1) – is to stress the interdependence of continuous additions to the running text. In the words of detective Lester Freamon in *The Wire*: "We're building something here . . . and all the pieces matter." This sentence, spoken within the narrative, simultaneously guides the act of narration because it lets viewers know how the series wants to be watched – and how it wants to be seen. Apparently, it has been successful on both counts, given the frequency with which this sentence is taken up and developed in critical articles.[51]

Thus, a pervasive topos in descriptions of *The Wire* holds that everything that happens in the narrative is somehow "connected" and "remembered," suggesting that all events follow the rules of a complicated but coherent plot or "game." These are key terms from the show's dialogues but also from scholarly analyses of the show: one description mobilizes the other. Memory, however, is a mechanism of retrospective selection, so it is quite challenging to imagine a narrative in which all happenings were actually remembered. As Mittell notes, establishing connectivity is a standard aspect of serial reception anyway.[52] And true, many effects of unity in *The Wire* are created retroactively, by taking up and explaining clues introduced earlier. Like any series, too, *The Wire* keeps accumulating clues and characters for later development – exactly in order to produce an effect of unity – without making use of all of them or with the same intensity of connection. At the end of Season Three, for instance, police commander Rawls is shown in a gay bar: a scene anticipating future plot strands and character continuations (or "revelations" in the show's logic of pre-established consistency) which, however, are never remembered to be developed.

This is not to minimize the range and sophistication of unity-building devices in *The Wire*. But I suggest that we view the show's interest in enacting the identity of a complex serial (rather than a sprawling series) as conflict-ridden. Even in its self-contained, crypto-novelistic structures – most notably in its canon-bound materialization as a closed DVD set, complete with modes of storytelling that count on exactly such a type of distribution and reception – *The Wire* generates evolving structures with a vested interest in reproduction: a "series" playing a "serial" (in the industry definition of these terms). Continuation is the name of the game, not just organization. Or put differently: The show's investment in the organization of complexity is inevitably bound up with the complications of serial proliferation.

While it can be ruled out that all sixty episodes existed in a pre-conceived state at the beginning of production in 2002 and were then simply canned over the next six years, without recursive work on their own effects, the series has good reasons to obscure its evolving structures and simulate an intricate consistency. *The Wire* achieves this brilliantly, both inside and outside its core narrative. It does so, for instance, by suggesting that, unlike *Deadwood, The Sopranos* et al., it is not a character-driven drama. Still, the narrative's focus on institutional entanglements cannot prevent the emergence of favorite characters among audiences, writers, or television actors. In 2012, an interesting effect of this development could be witnessed on David Simon's blog, *The Audacity of Despair*. Simon complained that a journalist asked President Obama, not about the social issues raised by *The Wire*, but about his favorite character on the show.[53] Simon's displeasure with this – as with other consequences of *The Wire* – is not untypical of the displeasures of serial authorship in general, because serial storytelling always challenges an author's sense of control over any message he or she means to convey. What is untypical, at least for commercial storytellers, is the tenacity with which Simon claims interpretive authority, rather than to integrate the displeasures of serial authorship – that is, the precariousness of personal power over what an ongoing narrative sets in motion – into the aesthetic doings of the series itself (as David Chase arguably did in the final season of *The Sopranos*). From the perspective of Actor-Network-Theory, one can say that journalists who ask about favorite characters, or fans who draw up character alignment charts, have not necessarily misunderstood *The Wire*, but that they are *doing* something which the narrative allows, perhaps even triggers, them to do. More than that, already Simon – when he acted in his role as creator (showrunner, writer, etc.) and when he co-created characters like Bubbles and Omar – *did* something that was suggested by culturally habituated modes of characterization and storytelling. Once a character like Omar is invented, his success (meaning the pleasures and profits he brings to viewers and producers alike) limits the possibilities of what can be successfully done "with" such a character, because the character itself suggests a spectrum of further narrative or performative choices which, if explored, might well *make* Bill Simmons ask Barack Obama about his favorite *Wire* character, whether David Simon later likes it or not.[54]

Such favorite characters, then, are always profitable for continuation. In fact, they are driving forces *of* continuation, deepened and developed in reaction to their popularity within and without the show, exerting more and more influence on the narrative. Omar and Bubbles are obvious examples, and it is telling how strongly Simon feels he has to deny that these figures evolved throughout the series – especially if such evolution is said to have been prompted by the interference of unauthorized forces (read viewers):

> We are cautious about allowing any feedback to induce us to appease or please viewers . . . [V]iewers generally don't know what is good for them as an audience, or for *The Wire*. . . . So I'm afraid we are not at all open to suggestion or petition when it comes to character or story.[55]

Such disclaimers are belied by their own rhetoric and the diegetic paths of the characters in question. It bears mention that Bubbles and Omar are by far the most romantic figures in a narrative otherwise intent on avoiding sentimental heroizing.

According to Alvarez, the actors playing these parts were told in the beginning that their characters would not last longer than seven or eight episodes. But then they "proved to be of service to the story."[56] Altogether, *The Wire's* acclaimed multiperspectivity is not fundamentally different from the pliability of conventional serial ensemble casts. Characterization in *The Wire* puts a premium on charisma and physical beauty (Stringer Bell, McNulty, Kima);[57] contrastive couplings are common (McNulty and Bunk, Stringer and Barksdale, etc.); free agents (Omar, Cutty) are positioned in heroic counterpoint to the constraints of institutional systems; "framing" figures map the show's moral universe (the Greek, Marlo, and the newspaper editors as "the natural endpoint[s]," respectively, for "corner culture," globalized capitalism, and media corruption).[58] Omar, the desperado, is clearly modeled on legendary Western characters, down to his shotgun, duster, and personal code without specification to what it entails. Omar's initial quirks – buying Honey Nut Cheerios in his pajamas – are considerably toned down in later seasons in favor of mythological resonances immediately comprehensible to a media-savvy audience. Simon told the actor to prepare for the role by watching *The Wild Bunch* and *The Man Who Shot Liberty Valance*. Similarly, Marlo emerges as a kind of Hannibal Lecter of the ghettoes, romanticized as a truly magnetic sociopath, charismatic individualism gone evil.

Thus, leading character types and constellations in *The Wire* are guided at least as much by the show's narrative requirements and needs for serial reproduction as by its social vision.[59] In fact, the very search for interconnectedness often strains and overstrains the limits of what is credible in terms of social realism. Characters undergo career changes and even personality alterations (presented as developments) that resemble the twists and turns of a soap opera – all in the service of tying together the proliferating settings through stable figures or economically finding new functions for old elements. Thus, Pryzbylewski becomes a teacher, which binds the world of the schools in Season Four to the police procedural of Season One; Herc somewhat implausibly becomes the mayor's protégé and then is hired by the gangsters' attorney Levy, etc.

Similar tensions are visible at the macro-level of season structure. Ultimately, the show's expansion onto ever more social institutions has a cumulative rather than systematic effect. In principle, there is no end to such movement; it could go on indefinitely: the very definition of a series.[60] This is to say that the ongoing narrative actually *performs complexity increase and complexity reduction simultaneously*, constantly bringing in new material and integrating it into what came before rather than devising a state of maximum density necessarily present in each partial description (the structural fiction behind Luhmann's oeuvre). A never realized sixth season was to explore the Hispanic side of Baltimore, absent in previous seasons and in no way needed for them to tell their stories of complexity. Before that, Seasons Four and Five introduced themes and characters meant to be deepened in a hypothetical tie-in series *The Hall*, centering on Mayor Carcetti.[61]

While aiming for the status and the practices of a unified oeuvre, the series thus remains structurally geared toward its own return and multiplication. Bringing to the flow of television the concentration and slow-down of self-contained works – and this with notable success – *The Wire* cannot help but engage in incessant movements forward and outward. Even its self-descriptions develop and accumulate in a serial fashion (competitive gestures directed both at network programs and *The Sopranos* are particularly resolute in Season One, the tragedy paradigm emerges with force in Season Two, etc.). In fact, the relationship of *The Wire* to Simon's earlier show *The Corner* and to his next television projects *Generation Kill* and *Treme* can be viewed in a similar manner.

If one privileges *The Wire*'s journalistic idea of itself, all of this can be explained as strategy, i.e., as the necessary but secondary practice of popular fiction enhancing the effectiveness of socio-logical reportage. I propose, however, that seriality is a major force in the cultural work of *The Wire*. The show's existence as a commercial series helps illuminate its presence in American culture, its interactions with its own receptions, its power to set in motion national discourses. To understand what *The Wire* is actually *doing* – to understand what it contributes to the culture it draws from – and to understand why this particular series has become the darling of contemporary American (media) studies, we need to take into account its momentous serial agency.

Consider this: The promise that everything is – or eventually will be – linked with everything else is a promise of ultimate closure. It is an attractive promise: In the end, all complications are captured in a big picture of high resolution. And this is what the series is actually doing, but doing it again and again, thus paradoxically. With each season finale, *The Wire* turns in onto itself and the remaining loose ends – which are really connecting options – fall into place. "We wrote for closure in case we weren't renewed," Simon explains a standard strategy of television story-telling.[62] But an ongoing series can make itself look like a closed work only in retrospect and its desire for reproduction is expunged not even then. Perhaps more than any other moment, therefore, in its six-year run, the finale of *The Wire* encapsulates its cultural ambitions. Of course, having a meaningful end at all, or implying the possibility of one, is an important prerequisite for any narrative to be perceived as a work of art. No canon-ization without a bound or finished text. But what an ending! By far the most frequent expression viewers used to characterize the extended wrap-up offered by the final minutes of Season Five was: "satisfying." Many a commentator added: It was satisfying because it was "unambiguous" – which meant to imply that it was exactly not like the ending of *The Sopranos*.[63]

It is an obvious but telling comparison. The finale of *The*

Sopranos (throwing viewers back onto the physically startling image of a blank television screen) reflected the series' awareness, perhaps loathing, of its own effects as serial entertainment at the time of the Iraq war.[64] *The Wire*, by contrast, treats its audience to "an almost absurdly exhaustive festival of closure," which, according to one viewer, "said with forcefulness: Life is definitely not fair, but it's well worth doing the hard work of living. . . . Power is essentially evil."[65] For a show that has often prided itself on being "bored with good and evil," this is remarkable.[66] But true: For *The Wire*, the performance of complexity amounts to paradoxically repeated attempts at what John Kraniauskas has called "narrative totalization."[67] Not only in its uneasy initial identity (as a police procedural with a difference), the show hopes to render uniform a dense and multilayered structure in which "all the pieces matter." As a series, too, it provides comforting reductions of the narrative complexities it has produced, and produced for the explicit purpose of organizing and reducing them.[68] Finally, in terms of subject matter, *The Wire* is busy organizing the intricacies and entanglements of urban life at the beginning of the 21st century into recognizable patterns – patterns that can be serially reproduced in follow-up narratives, stories within and without the serial text, sociological interpretations, political convictions, ideological positions, rallying cries of identification. *The Wire* makes followers.

2

Hetero-Descriptions

Stories can be organized as self-contained structures, as if they were necessitated by the very experience of art they afford, but no story exists in self-sufficient artistic isolation. Serial stories, in particular, with their feedback loops of production and reception, are force-fields of connection. They activate practices and mobilize practitioners far beyond their textual bounds. Thus, in turning now to scholarly discussions of *The Wire*, my aim is not to map the self-descriptions identified in Chapter One onto the field of academic discourse. My point is not that (American) scholarship merely repeats the show's images of itself but that it continues the conflicts present in these images into national arenas of self-identification.

Of course, to read public readings of *The Wire* as active within the narrative's own cultural work complicates many of the certainties put forward by the series and its observers. This, however, is not meant as a way of "exposing" scholarship's "complicity" in this or that ideological hazard of *The Wire*. Rather, I wish to track how American (media) studies participate in the activities of their objects – or more ambitiously put: how American (media) studies and American (media) practices act as interdependent forces of a larger cultural system calling itself (against all odds in these supposedly post-national times) American culture.

Why this stress on America? It is a fact well known but worth repeating that scholars of contemporary texts are always doing more than simply analyzing those texts, especially when they operate within and on the same environment as their texts – which is the case when American media scholars examine American television or, for that matter, when Americanists from the United States produce knowledge about America. Whatever else their goals and results, these types of study are always also acts of cultural self-description – and they can be analyzed as such, to trace dependencies between a culture's knowledge and performance of itself, ideally from a perspective not directly contributing to such self-identifications.[69]

The question, then, is not simply why *The Wire* has generated so much admiration among academic commentators, but which shapes this admiration takes, which transactions it stimulates, which debates and assurances it enables. Needless to say, few of the positions identified in the following can be attributed unambiguously to single contributions that would contain no other dispositions. But there are some pervasive trades between *The Wire* and its readings in the United States and other English-speaking countries. (Some divergences between US and non-US analyses will be discussed toward the end of this chapter.) I distinguish the following moves: selective duplication, downward identification, activist concern, upward recognition, and analytical dislocation.

Selective Duplication

In its thematic selections and interpretive interests, English-language scholarship on *The Wire* is to a large degree dependent on prior discussions in the press and on the web. These journalistic and para-journalistic discussions, in turn, exhibit a pronounced tendency to duplicate isolated self-descriptions of the series, relying on David Simon's interviews, HBO public relations material, other journalistic pieces, etc. Such circularity certainly reflects the time pressures of daily text production. But self-reinforcing as these communications are, they do more than simply repeat the show's interests. Rather, they serve to *speed up* its cultural activities. By condensing discordant aesthetic identities into easily reproducible meanings and quick formulas ("televised novel," "complexity," "authenticity," etc.), they may diminish their object's aesthetic density, but what *The Wire* loses in terms of experiential wealth it gains in terms of public effectiveness. Commonplaces culled from the series' repertoire of identifications give currency to its text, turning it into a versatile object of public exchange.

At first glance, it would seem inappropriate for scholarship to engage in this kind of reductionism. It would seem more fitting to trace the show's simultaneous buildup and diminution of complexity rather than to perpetuate auto-references with regard to only one side of the equation. But then, studies of popular culture are by definition confronted with a confusing array of daily growing material. They are continually challenged to bring informational order to such proliferation. Often working as archivists of the present, scholars of commercial culture are under an obligation to document "what is out there" – which can result in analyses that read like consumer reports with a cultural studies vocabulary.

Even so, when academic publications (under which category I include everything published with an affiliation to institutions of higher learning) duplicate statements from the series' paratexts, they often transform them into statements of fact or treat them as if they were results of analysis. Sometimes quoting David Simon verbatim, without always acknowledging or realizing that they are doing so, contributions maintain that "In *The Wire* there is no such thing as good and evil as clear-cut moral categories," "The structure of the programme itself is that of an epic novel," "[*The Wire* is] a modernized and American version of Greek Tragedy," "Simon was writing a televised novel, and a big one," etc.[70] In particular, statements about the complexity of *The Wire* have taken on a mantra-like quality, paradoxically draining the term "complexity" of complexity.[71]

Such reductive duplications help to assimilate *The Wire* in a more or less fixed manner to public and scholarly convictions, many of them perpetuating the series' own narratives and attachments. In this way, competing (political, epistemological, even theological, etc.) positions can deploy *The Wire* as an exemplification of their own assumptions and beliefs. The serial text is turned into an intermediary for public contest, a stable currency for dissimilar purchases: *The Wire*, we read, "illuminates," "embodies," "reveals," "harmonizes with" ideas of critical pedagogy, urban development theory, "theoretical conceptions of black masculinity," libertarian conservatism, "Marx's critical engagement with primitive accumulation," "Catholic teaching in the 20th century [and] readings from church documents," Paul Tillich's "structure of hope," "the core insight of social network analysis," Human Resource Management, "the roles and behaviours of managers in the UK's National Health Service," etc.[72]

Sociological and ethnographic approaches in particular have absorbed the series' claims to realism, not so much attempting sociological or ethnographic analyses of *The Wire*, but using *The Wire* to illustrate their own methods and results. In fact, the majority of examples quoted above is taken from the collection *The Wire: Urban Decay and American Television* and the conference *"The Wire* as Social Science Fiction?", organized by the Leeds Centre for Research on Socio-Cultural Change in the UK. Both ventures declare that they are interested in the connections of *The Wire* to the social sciences, especially urban sociology. However, with a few telling exceptions, contributors understand such connections not in terms of mutual dealings between the series and urban sociology (texts contextualizing each other) but in terms of the show's use-value *for* urban sociology. The ruling assumption is that there exists a socio-historical background of facts which is then represented – reported, in fact – in the show's surface narrative. Hence, *The Wire* can be employed as a convenient short-cut to observing social life in action: "a useful visual tool for . . . criminologists," "the best ethnographic text on the US today," or even "an illustrative example of the kind of non-fictional case study that social scientists might ideally aspire to."[73]

This last description is interesting for the chiasmus it performs. If I understand the argument correctly, it likens *The Wire* to a veritable case study of social life, while the show's narrative power is held up as a model for sociological writing. Unwittingly, such acceptance of *The Wire*'s documentary ambitions highlights the fictional base of many social science accounts – especially in the United States, it should be added, where these accounts are in intense competition for public attention and political relevance. The actual exchanges between sociology and *The Wire*, which are visible in such publications, invite investigation into the narrative dimension of sociological knowledge production itself.[74]

For the actors involved, however, such mutuality mostly serves as a source of embarrassment, given the compulsive manner in which they return to the fiction/fact dynamics and try to collapse one term into the other. When William J. Wilson and Anmol Chaddha taught *The Wire* in a sociology class at Harvard – a move guaranteed to draw some public attention – they explained their motivation as follows: "[Teaching about] urban inequality . . . we get some help from Bodie, Stringer Bell, Bubbles, and others. . . . [*The Wire*] shows ordinary people making sense of their world."[75]

Wilson's participation in this use of the series is interesting because Wilson's sociological work has criticized popular media for covering urban poverty as a problem of individual lifestyles ("culture of poverty"), with little room left for narratives and images that stress systemic conditions or larger economic frameworks.[76] Thus, Wilson is very much aware of fiction's power to shape social attitudes, and he is in a good position to recognize – and applaud – *The Wire*'s achievements in challenging representational conventions of race and class.[77] All the more striking is his and other sociologists' readiness to downplay the fabricated character of a commercial story-world that is an active player in the very society they are investigating. One explanation for this blind spot is that many American sociologists actually recognize their own work dramatized in the series. In a long essay published in *Critical Inquiry*, Chaddha and Wilson claim that *The Wire* "effectively illustrates the fundamental nature of systemic urban inequality."[78] It does so, they hold, by undermining the emphasis on individual action that is so deeply ingrained in American (media) attitudes toward poverty – a reading partly contradicted, partly qualified, by other audience responses, such as Linda Williams's interpretation (published in the same issue of *Critical Inquiry*), which discusses *The Wire* as a melodrama with ethnographic ambitions, highly dependent for its efficiency on viewers' empathy and identification with individual characters.

In another contribution to the *Critical Inquiry* discussion, Kenneth Warren can therefore declare that Chaddha and Wilson's praise of *The Wire* "might seem somewhat self-congratulatory" given that they use the show as a vehicle for presenting their own brand of sociology when they juxtapose detailed research reports with – rather cursory – references to plot elements and character constellations.[79] (The structure of Chaddha and Wilson's survey also follows the thematic structure of the show's first four seasons: "Crime and Incarceration," "Joblessness and Work," "Politics and Urban Policy," "Education and Youth.") But then, Simon himself has cited Wilson's *When Work Disappears* as an inspiration for the show (as Warren also points out).[80] In fact, quite a few of the descriptions of American society produced by *The Wire* correspond in obvious ways with – and are even actively informed by – self-studies of American society in urban sociology, especially the Chicago School in the wake of Robert Park.[81] Little wonder that Chaddha and Wilson can watch the series with a sense of almost total recognition. But Warren, in his alternative reading, is not interested in charting the actual traffic between Chicago-style sociology, ethnographic journalism, and cable TV storytelling within a larger system of American self-descriptions. After accurately stating that US urban sociology is involved in the social realities it observes and critiques, he goes on to blame Wilson's sociological work for having contributed, if indirectly, to the displacement of the urban poor under President Clinton's HOPE VI program – despite Wilson's endorsement of basically ordoliberalist, even Social Democratic measures, far removed from the neoliberalism of Clinton's welfare policies.[82]

What is really at stake, then, in the increasingly impassioned exchange between Warren and Wilson/Chaddha is a schism within left-wing American self-studies itself: a schism between more Marxist and more culturalist accounts of urban inequality. In the heat of the argument, this schism sporadically boils down to a standoff between class-oriented and race-oriented analysis, and the success of an argument rests on the vigor with which it can establish itself as more "critical" and less "complicit" than its competitor.[83] The good fight is fought here not so much over *The Wire* as by deploying *The Wire* for predetermined commitments and convictions.[84] Thus, Warren claims to have found in Chaddha and Wilson's article a "misreading" of the series, but what he actually objects to is an alleged misinterpretation of sociological data – as if *The Wire* provided exactly that. To a certain extent, each party in this quarrel sees something important about its antagonist (Warren critiquing Chaddha and Wilson for "bring[ing] poverty and its depiction in *The Wire* under the regime of sociology"; Chaddha and Wilson observing that "Warren's objection is that our essay does not advance his preferred view of how politics figures in urban poverty and inequality"),[85] but both remain disinclined to examine the shared assumptions that lock them into competitive positions. More than that, both frankly ignore the versions of *The Wire* produced by other participants in the same debate. Somewhat surprisingly, for example, Chaddha and Wilson identify Linda Williams's contribution, which argues that the series needs to be addressed as a fictional media text, as a "supplement to our essay."[86] Since this is all they say about it, the key point of aesthetic readings seems to have eluded them.

This is remarkable, because sociological interest in the show's realism conflicts in a number of ways with the show's empirical identity as a television series. To begin with, and contrary to the words of Wilson and Chaddha's syllabus, Stringer Bell and Omar are hardly "ordinary," nor are they "people." To be able to treat them as people, i.e., to use television series as "new fictional sources," sociologists and ethnographers have to explain the text's practice of storytelling as insignificant for their research interests.[87] Strategies to do so include: talking about fiction not as a set of multi-authored social acts but as a finished, one-time *translation* of reality into a textual medium;[88] conceding that *The Wire* is fiction, but then proceeding as if it were not (summarizing plot lines as evidence of what is wrong with municipal politics, talking about Carcetti as if he was the real mayor of a real city, etc.);[89] taking up Simon's suggestion that narrative is a *tactic* in the service of social reportage;[90] claiming that the show is reflexively "blurring the boundaries" between fact and fiction, but concluding that in doing so it establishes some kind of "superior story" that weds the emotive force of narrative to the authenticity of documentation.[91]

These uses of *The Wire* single out specific self-descriptions at the expense of others, mostly drawing on the show's journalistic identity as promoted by Simon. On the one hand, this attests to the text's cultural force, its ability to contribute to ongoing social debates. On the other hand, the activities of the series are limited to those that can be easily assimilated to the viewer's own chosen sphere of action. In principle, there is nothing wrong with that; one can always legitimize such limitation as a matter of research interest and focus. But the series' other activities will not be put to rest. What is more, they carry on *within* the exclusions of such allegorical readings, opening them in turn for (self-)investigation and ultimately challenging the scientific range of methods unable or unwilling to engage in such investigation. A sociologist who excludes the agency of fiction from her understanding of American society – or an Americanist who regards TV narratives as illustrative mirrors rather than influential makers of American culture – will almost certainly produce insufficient knowledge, and quite unnecessarily so. In the end, to duplicate *The Wire*'s claims to realism serves to confirm what a discipline already knows about reality. Such duplications invite questions about the culture-making force of fiction itself: questions about where the prior knowledge that guides these observations actually comes from. Self-confirmation through media artifacts paradoxically tends to disconfirm scholarship's own sense of realism.

Downward Identification

If some of the readings quoted above appear more plausible than others, this is because they stay close to what is already known about the series. Transforming auto-references into external observations, they exhibit a strong tendency toward self-confirmation, both concerning an observer's explicitly held convictions and the veracity of public knowledge in general. Have local witnesses repeat often enough that *The Wire* looks exactly like Baltimore and this will become a matter of experiential fact even for people who have never visited the city or lived in it.

However, stories mobilize not only knowledge but also sentiments. They are forces of conviction and identification alike, able to substantiate what is already held but also to bring near what is emotively distant (or to configure what they bring near as new feelings). In this regard, one of the main achievements of *The Wire* is how it inverts entrenched routines of racial representation on American television. Featuring a majority of African American characters (rather than the token ethnic representative typical of American ensemble casts), arranging them over a wide social spectrum of shifting moral properties (rather than focusing on one class and affirming middle-class values even in depictions of the urban poor), and portraying members of the black underclass as individualized subjects of ambiguous actions (rather than objects of police work or sentimental victims), the show is engaged in a "de-centering of whiteness" unusual in contemporary popular entertainment.[92]

Some critical discussions are content to register this politics of representation and to approve its motives. More accept the show's invitation to identify with its underclass characters and continue the emotive work of *The Wire* into scholarship. Only a few contributions raise questions about this type of identification, and when they do, it is usually to stress their own privileged association with the social world presented or to distance themselves from what they perceive as illegitimate appropriations.

In all these cases, the affiliation of academic scholars with inner-city characters displays strong traits of downward identification, no matter the ethnic or social origin of the writer in question. In fact, most scholars are acutely aware of their present remoteness from the world shown in *The Wire* and, significantly, perceive it as a deficit to be explained, excused, or neutralized. This puts them under constant pressure to state their own relations to a (representation of) social reality explicitly removed from their own.

Alignment between reader and characters can be achieved in a number of ways. One rare example, published in the *Journal of Speculative Philosophy*, selects a particular figure (Omar) and sets him up as a model that can be emulated in situations socially distant but ideally close to the daily struggles of middle- and upper-class biographies: "we Omar wannabes" can draw on this "free spirit . . . who live[s] unconcerned with what others expect" in order to fight our own "unending battle with the *status quo*."[93] At the other end of the spectrum are descriptions that turn characters more or less openly into *objects of desire*, as in a gay reading that applauds the show's "eroticization of the hood."[94]

To understand why the series is able to push the boundaries of narrative into ever wider fields of public practice, it is important to see how its emotive offerings encourage readers to write themselves into the story and to publicly behave like characters of the show. Not a few scholars simulate closeness to their favorite fictional gangsters and junkies by reproducing their slang in the middle of critical analysis, freely quoting from their sayings, or referring to them like old acquaintances – which for all practical purposes, as serial characters, they are. Another, more powerful, strategy is to establish one's autobiographical credentials as an African American, Baltimorean, former member of the proletariat, minority speaker, etc., all the while reproducing the show's insistence that privileged access yields authentic knowledge (not "where you're at" counts but "where you're from").[95]

Accordingly, at the 2009 conference in Leeds, the participants from Baltimore were scheduled early in the program. Similarly, the collection *Urban Decay and American Television*, after gently cautioning in its introduction against the "documentary fallacy," offers as its first contribution the memoir of a former inhabitant of Baltimore's Eastside, now a published poet and holder of an endowed chair of English, who reminisces about the people that inspired leading gangland characters in *The Wire*. He creatively refers to them by their fictional names: "[Proposition] Joe and I were attending junior high school at the same time. We might have known each other. . . . When Omar was a young teenager in the mid-1980s . . . I was a blue-collar worker in the city before going off to Brown University's creative writing program."[96] Prolonging the serial narrative into his recollections of the city, the writer includes himself in the fictional story-world ("Proposition Joe and I") – a move that draws attention both to the lived relevance of *The Wire*'s urban representations and to the operations of fiction in any sort of temporal self-identification. According to the same logic, self-consciously white writers can name themselves as such, admitting that their attitude to the show is guided by a need for "sharing" and calling this need "white" (but then quoting "my friend Winston," presumably an African American, to authenticate the speaker's position).[97] In another turn, self-consciousness about self-consciousness can yield irony, as in Christian Lander's – not exactly scholarly but obliquely critical – inclusion of *The Wire* in *Stuff White People Like*, a compendium of taste more revealing about class-bound and national embarrassments than ethnic ones.[98] This confessional mode is not restricted to American writers who identify as members of larger groups in order to tap into – or mock – the show's group-intensive gratifications; it easily crosses national borders, at least into other English-speaking countries.[99]

Evidently, all these identifications depend on the assumption that *The Wire* paints an accurate picture of race and class in Baltimore and, by extension, America. The series itself stresses its documentary credentials by reminding viewers again and again that single events are based on "true stories" "heard by" Simon (the truth of the story residing exactly in the fact that it was heard by, and most probably told to, a reporter).[100] Casting policy, too, provides much-publicized proof of credibility. Not only are approximately 65% of the cast black, but many characters are actually played by amateurs from Baltimore, some of them real-life inspirations for other parts, some of them "real gangsters," in that revealing conjunction of reality and outlaw existence popular in American storytelling.[101] The two most famous correlations between Baltimore people and serial figures are convicted murderer Felicia "Snoop" Pearson playing the character of Snoop, and the marriage of Don Andrews (reportedly a model for Omar) and Fran Boyd (a former junkie and informant for Simon's *The Corner*), described in one academic article as "a real-life fulfillment of the promise the series at times presents to the viewer."[102] In striking contrast, three leading characters, McNulty, Stringer Bell, and Tommy Carcetti, are played by English and Irish actors who first had to learn how to speak with a Baltimore accent.

These eye-catching "blurrings" of the fact/fiction divide are frequently read as reflexive gestures, in which the series "raises some issues surrounding the notions of performance, authenticity, and 'otherness'."[103] However, in terms of their foreignness to Baltimore, there is little self-reflection in Dominic West's performance of McNulty and none in Idris Elba's of Stringer Bell or Aidan Gillen's of Carcetti. On the contrary, the naturalistic styles of these actors significantly reinforce the series' feel of realism. More interesting than their nationality, then, is the reason why they were selected in the first place. Simon says he switched to British players for the parts of McNulty and Stringer Bell because all Americans who auditioned for the roles had watched too many American cop shows and copied them in their performances.[104]

This is a revealing statement and it rhymes with *The Wire*'s media philosophy. To a large degree, the show's effect of authenticity depends on canceling the presence of American television from its representational identity. To make a convincing case for realism, *The Wire* has to subtract its own (medium's) activities from the social world it depicts. In this sense, to have a gangster played by an actor unspoiled by American television corresponds with the decision to represent Baltimore's social reality as one in which television plays no part. *The Wire* treats its viewers to a world in which cops and criminals are blissfully ignorant of, and thoroughly uninfluenced by, the ways cops and criminals behave on TV – an assumption actually shared with most conventional television drama: realism at the expense of realistic self-representation.[105] Unlike many of its HBO competitors, then, *The Wire* has remarkably little to say about television. Apart from a few inside jokes that serve to underline the show's distance both from traditional series and other quality programs (when a gangster prefers network fare to *Deadwood* or when another points to the self-referential absurdity of *Dexter*), watching television does not feature as a social practice in *The Wire*. When the media finally do play a role in Season Five, the question is significantly one of representation versus misrepresentation: The final season suggests that the decline of journalism is epitomized by reporters making things up. The underlying assumption is that the media *convey* reality, either correctly or incorrectly, and since *The Wire*'s own claims to realism are strongly tied to the notion of accurate translation, the show has no interest in treating the media, including itself, as actively shaping the things they represent. In this fashion, the deceits of the fictional *Baltimore Sun* which are told about *in* the narrative ultimately emphasize the veracity *of* the narrative's own naturalistic reportage – in the same manner in which the wrap-up finale reinforces the series' striving for narrative totality.

Such discrepancies have led one sociologist to invite "real thugs" to watch the show with him – and write about it in a nine-part article series for the *Freakonomics* blog linked on the *New York Times* website. Sudhir Venkatesh's experiment and its rhetoric deserve an analysis of their own. I shall restrict my remarks to saying that the gangsters' engagement with *The Wire*, as filtered through Venkatesh (a former student of William J. Wilson), points at once to the idealized nature of the series' narrative and to the ways in which this narrative mobilizes emotionally charged self-performances among those reportedly represented. For example, Venkatesh's gangsters would like to see more winners and losers in the story, not everyone defeated (which they take to be typical for a narrative authored by a white writer), more sex, especially between black and white characters, more dominant female characters in the ghetto, less concession to the serial demands of suspense and revenge plots ("In the ghetto, you never have this kind of thing last so long. People kill each other right away, or not at all"), and less stress on the complexity of business transactions ("The one thing I don't like about this show is you never make plans when you're hustling. Not for more than a few days anyway").[106] The self-described "rogue sociologist" looks on to report dangerous knowledge gleaned from the show and "a group of gangland acquaintances," now operating as if in unison as a collective actor. Noting that *The Wire* "accorded with my own fieldwork in Chicago and New York," Venkatesh claims that watching it with "a few respected street figures" is the best way "to ensure quality control." Confirming the results of fieldwork through fieldwork on his informants' reactions to what he takes to be an illustrative version of these results, Venkatesh winds up suspended between amused monitoring and representations of toughness that surpass even *The Wire*'s claims to brutal authenticity. Dutifully reminding his informants that it is only a TV show (when one of their favorite characters is killed) does not get him out of this tautological round – perhaps the problem is in the word "only" – but further into it: "I was thrown a 'f–k you' stare that only men with deep knowledge of hand-to-hand combat could give."[107] Deep knowledge about rough existence: Venkatesh's hardboiled rhetoric marks downward identification as a dead serious matter.

Activist Concern

Among academic readings of *The Wire*, there is one small group which deviates from the generally admiring tone of scholarship. These contributions largely share the show's interest in reportage but question its correctness and effects. Assessing the series against the background of its own critique of capitalism, they hold that *The Wire* does little to mend or counteract the social conditions it so forcefully condemns.

The first sustained – and, to date, most nuanced – formulation of this argument appeared not in a scholarly article but in Bowden's 2008 essay in *The Atlantic*. Bowden quotes Yale sociologist Elijah Anderson, author of such studies as *A Place on the Corner, Streetwise* and *Code of the Streets*, who called the series "an exaggeration. I get frustrated watching it." Bowden concurs: "[Simon's] political passions ultimately trump his commitment to accuracy or evenhandedness." Taking up Anderson's diagnosis of "a bottom-line cynicism" in *The Wire*, he describes the series as "relentlessly . . . *bleak*."[108]

Remarkably, this critique, too, draws on one of the show's auto-referential topoi, if disapprovingly so. The term "bleak," habitually reproduced after Bowden's article to mark the series' more disillusioned aspects, calls to mind (and was probably inspired by) Charles Dickens's *Bleak House*. Similarly, some scholars complain about the "fatalism" of social vision in *The Wire*, acknowledging the narrative's self-definition as Greek tragedy updated for postmodern times.[109] Almost all these readings accept David Simon as the authoritative source of textual meaning (in the case of Bowden even explaining central features of the narrative as results of the author's mental conflicts). Altogether, they function like special cases of the sociological duplications described above, singling out separate images of the series, accelerating them in public discourse, but this time not to ally themselves with them but to formulate distinct counter-narratives.

Counter-narratives have a way of illuminating deep-seated contradictions of the stories they are written against. In this, they can be sharp tools of analysis.[110] At the same time, to tell a story with the explicit purpose of proving another story wrong usually presupposes commitments of a more systematic kind than expressed even by the term "conviction." Such dedicated critiques are often spoken from the position of exceptionally strong and extensive obligations, like a religious faith or a formalized political ideology: super-narratives which confront other texts not only with an impulse of integrating them but as direct rivals in world-explanation. Thus, to complain that the society presented in *The Wire* is "irredeemable" – a key term among concerned activists – means to hold a vision, and probably a plan, of social redemption.[111] In its more pragmatic form, focused on concrete troubles in concrete localities, this type of critique combines praise for *The Wire*'s ability to "raise awareness" with indictment of its failure "to offer any understanding that the problems facing cities and the urban poor are *solvable*."[112]

It is a normative project, both in its doctrinaire and its reformist shape. These readings would want to *change* the text. "What is needed," one critic writes, is to take up "the moral appeal of [Simon's] tragic argument" but employ it for "additional engagements" and "affirmative articulations of political and social problems capable of transforming the tragic conditions of the city."[113] Ultimately, this amounts to blaming the series for what it is, advocating readings that are not just different from existing ones but hoping for different narratives to replace it. Again, there is nothing wrong with that; it is an incentive to cultural production. But as scholarship, these readings show little interest in investigating the real work done by a real narrative. At their most extreme, they reduce actions to an agenda. Their continuation of the series is instrumental, often attempting to discontinue what they see as its harmful effects.

Small wonder, then, that activist accounts approach textual structures in a decidedly selective manner. They note, correctly, that the final episode shows how social roles reproduce themselves "fatalistically" through new agents (Michael takes Omar's position, Dukie becomes a second Bubbles, Sydnor replaces McNulty) but ignore that McNulty and Bubbles "go home" in the end, and how this has prompted many a commentator to describe the finale as highly satisfying and life affirming. One viewer's bleakness is another viewer's hope. But it is possible to ask how such discrepancies can exist at all, how the narrative enables these dissimilar effects, and what the co-presence of closure and continuation tells us about the serial text, its cultural doings, and the culture it helps sustain.

While activist readings challenge the accuracy of *The Wire* – an "exaggeration," says Anderson; no community activists, no black working class in this fictional Baltimore, say others[114] – they accord with the case-study approach of Venkatesh and other sociologists in excluding the productivity of mass-media storytelling from their notion of social reality. Consider that the inversion of racial and hetero-normative stereotypes in and by *The Wire* already has an activist dimension. Designing an openly homosexual outlaw character like Omar may not be a feat of social realism but it is a forceful intervention in the representational customs of American television.[115] This is true for many characterizations and constellations in *The Wire*: they work on existing social (media) practices. To ignore this means to regard these practices not as practices at all but as handy symbols of social realities to which they are true or not.

In turn, concerns about the activist value of *The Wire* have affected the show's self-understanding, probably even before they were first voiced by external observers. The makers of *The Wire* are, by necessity, highly sensitive to charges of social irresponsibility, because the uniqueness of their product rests to a large extent on its claims of political dissent. For Simon, something even more personal is at stake, after Season Five's thinly veiled attacks on Bill Marimow and John Carroll, senior editors of *The Baltimore Sun*, have backfired into a debate about different types of journalism. At heart, this debate is about effective and ineffective forms of social commitment. The *Columbia Journalism Review*, interviewing both sides, pointedly concludes that there is indeed a difference "between Simon's broad sociological approach and the rifle-shot approach taken by Carroll and Marimow, and rewarded all over the country by the Pulitzer board: the latter approach demonstrably affects – possibly even saves – individual lives."[116]

Perhaps the stubbornness with which *The Wire*, despite its proclaimed boredom with moral dichotomies, takes sides against bad institutions, bad corporations, bad superiors, bad elites, and bad Emmy committees, compensates for a feeling of comparative futility. As if hoping for a purpose that would channel the diffuse serial proceedings of their creation into more targeted kinds of action, six writers for *The Wire* issued a statement on March 5, 2008 (over Time/CNN no less) in which they declared "War on the Drug War" by the following means: "If asked to serve on a jury deliberating a violation of state or federal drug laws, we will vote to acquit, regardless of the evidence presented." Associating the "American dissent" of "jury nullification" with Thomas Paine's somewhat inaccurately summarized spirit of "civil disobedience against monarchy," they brought out heavy artillery for an unlikely fight.[117] I suggest that we read this resolution, explicitly connected to *The Wire* in its title and marketing, as the re-entry of activist concerns into serial self-observation. Serial producers, too, have an interest in keeping their product handy and controlling unpredictable ideological sprawl.

Upward Recognition

In addition to the readings discussed so far, *The Wire* has attracted, as all cultural artifacts seem destined to do, interpretations inspired by large explanatory systems commonly classified as Theory. I am talking about model-type academic discourses with ambitions of virtually unlimited applicability. Sometimes correlated with formalized beliefs or explicit political convictions, they are not necessarily determined by a social agenda nor bound by disciplinary methods (as is the case-study definition of *The Wire* described above). Instead, Theory aspires to an essentially philosophical project of truth, even when it claims to have left behind such notions, typically justifying its performative contradictions by declaring that any transcendence requires repetition of the thing to be transcended. Highly dependent on the charisma of individual master-thinkers – and their names – Theory offers to the time-pressed humanities an attractive repertoire of argumentative short-cuts both prestigious (because of their performed depth and difficulty) and efficient (because of their secure reproducibility, once mastered). In scholarship on *The Wire*, the writings of Michel Foucault, Gilles Deleuze, and to a lesser degree Jean Baudrillard and Guy Debord are the most active such models. A typical proposition reads:

> [*The Wire* is] the most Foucauldian show on television, the show which reveals the most about the technologies and techniques of contemporary discipline and punishment. We can map Foucault's theories about institutions fairly directly onto the Baltimore presented in *The Wire*, demonstrating how his ideas about power and discipline remain vitally important for social theory.[118]

The logic of this passage, representative of much critical practice in this vein, is tautological: The reader deploys Foucault to make sense of the narrative, then finds the narrative to mirror Foucault's "ideas" (this is not only a Foucauldian reading but the series itself is Foucauldian), and finally concludes that such agreement indicates the accuracy of these ideas. While the phrase "the Baltimore presented in *The Wire*" suggests that the object is, in fact, a media artifact, the distinction between artifact and exegetic tool is collapsed again in the concluding "demonstration" that Foucault's ideas are important for social theory *because* they are present in a television series. The question is: important in which ways? To understand what is happening here, consider that this passage is not interested in asking how and why Foucauldian notions of power have entered American commercial narratives. Rather, their presence there proves these notions to be correct.

On the one hand, this is another approach that takes for granted that *The Wire* "offers a comprehensive, faithful portrait of contemporary urban life, an essential case study for any theory of social organization."[119] On the other hand, Theory readings, judging by their argumentative economy, are less interested in illuminating the conditions of inner-city life with the help of televisual illustrations than they are in proclaiming that "the truth of [Foucault]" is "nowhere else in contemporary culture . . . so apparent as in *The Wire*."[120] The rhetorical thrust is clear, repeatedly juxtaposing scenes from the show with authoritative quotations from the master-texts: "In *Discipline and Punish*, Foucault describes how . . .," "*The Wire* confirms another of Foucault's maxims: . . .," "law enforcement as depicted in *The Wire*" exemplifies and ultimately proves "[a]n axiom of Foucault's theory of discipline," so that the series "merely illustrates with surprising accuracy his argument."[121] These scenes of recognition establish the narrative as a powerful allegory, connecting it upward to nothing less than axiomatic truth.

So far, I have found no readings that would trace the actual trades between this truth's content and the self-descriptions of *The Wire*. However, given the ease with which Foucault's texts can be applied to the series' social vision, it seems likely that the plausibility of these applications rests on more than just their philosophical aura. McMillan points to the narrative's "affinity with the social theory of Michel Foucault," but then refrains from investigating the terms and conditions of this affinity by declaring that "in [a] general sense, the concerns of Foucault and *The Wire* are identical."[122] What is meant is that Foucault's concerns include, like a framework, the concerns of the series. This reading essentially distinguishes between two *types* of texts, one offering a philosophical truth, the other playing out the philosophy's maxims as story.

It is the second type of text, the narrative, which is seen as doing something, but its doings are serviceable to the conceptual showings of the first type. All of this is quite in accordance with philosophical models of textuality which regard a text's practices (its rhetoric, its local involvements, its historical dealings) as part of its ephemeral or coincidental nature, necessarily inferior to the limitless (universal) propositions of Thought. To deprive Foucault's writings in this manner of their cultural occupations – their rhetorical business connections – means to privilege them as unmoved movers behind the busy exchanges of storytelling. This even works with philosophies that speak up for dissemination and currency, such as those of Derrida or Deleuze. Conversely, a television series associated with such meta-narratives can participate in the prestige of timeless writing: *The Wire* is "not simply great television, but *great art*," we read, because it does more than mimic social reality: it dramatizes its essence.[123]

If the narrative deviates too conspicuously from the axioms of the philosophical framework, there are a number of possibilities to account for this: One can proclaim a counter-truth of fiction that is said to "resist" such theoretical reduction (a position not yet established in the literature, as far as I can see).[124] Alternatively, one can limit one's descriptions to those elements that harmonize with the master-theory. For example, McMillan grounds his notion of victorious institutions and failed heroism in a quite partial – "Platonic" – concept of heroism, disregarding the presence of existentialist modes of heroic perseverance in *The Wire* (well documented in audience reactions that privilege the theme of individualism).

In addition, one can describe the narrative as differentiating, modifying, or extending the theoretical framework (preferably extending it onto other master-theories). Thus, McMillan enhances his Foucauldian reading by saying that *The Wire* redefines the modern totality of surveillance for the more fluent conditions of postmodern society. He explains that the show depicts individuals subverting the "panopticum," but in doing so they are creating their own networks of surveillance. Thus, the neoliberal weakening of central institutions is reintegrated, via Deleuze and Guattari's concept of machinic "assemblages," into a Foucauldian allegory of all-powerful institutions (somewhat forgetful of Foucault's own lectures on neoliberalism and anti-statism).[125]

Similarly, and finally, one can align the narrative with the doctrines of another master-thinker and have it engage in a truth struggle by proxy. The dialogic nature of this strategy invites examinations more dynamic than those offered by an integrative single-truth model. Thus, a suggestive reading of the show sets Foucault's motif of the panopticum in critical exchange with Debord's concept of the spectacle. Correctly noting that surveillance in *The Wire* is a messy and often futile affair, Joseph Schaub finds the series to be about "the failure of disciplinary surveillance" because it privileges the "low-tech gaze" of patient observation over the power of high-tech control. Possibly helped by the comparative informality of Debord's concept, Schaub can utilize this insight for descriptions which are relatively uncommitted to framework axioms but sensitive to the particularities of media (and other) effects. Thus, the spectacle's affinity to "narcissism" allows investigation into *The Wire*'s relations to contemporary docudramas and reality TV – and, theoretically, to itself and its audiences.[126]

The productivity of Theory-inspired readings in literary, media, and cultural studies is immense. With the help of their philosophical framework model of textuality, even secondary insights can be granted master-theoretical status, for example when the constructive role of institutions in identity-formation is presented as "Foucault's truth" or when an approach is called Foucauldian merely for maintaining that relations of power are important in social life. *The Wire* actually shares many of these insights, but it may have arrived at them by other routes, some of them possibly intersecting with the American activities and translations of Foucault's texts.[127] Ultimately, this raises the question of how these intersections are being traveled and by whom, which narratives and assumptions are shared or developed, and which transactions between *The Wire,* American sociology, and other truth agencies are actually taking place.

To enable such descriptions, it seems useful to accord to one's objects and tools alike the status of culturally effective interactors. Narratives exist not as phenomena in need of model explanations, but explanatory models are implicated in our narrative worlds, and both are probably better served by continuous lateral association than upward recognition. However, to make such associations – and to respect their continuities – requires a degree of self-awareness, not to mention breadth of contextualization, usually not available to individual writers but accessible only in the collective effects of mutual observation. A less costly and time-consuming method is enacted by a fifth class of approaches.

Analytical Dislocation

Analysis – understood as attention being paid to the ways in which interrelated parts construct or simulate a whole – can dislocate an object from the knowledge it holds and distributes about itself. Through this, analysis can disarticulate commonplaces in favor of critical redescriptions, breaking habits of meaning-making by making them explicit. Readings of *The Wire* that put such concerns center stage are obviously close to the approach chosen by and for this study. This makes it more difficult for me to bring to bear an analytical perspective on them, but a few patterns can be discerned.

In general, analytical redescription is always more likely to challenge than to accept *The Wire*'s depictions of itself, regardless of their adequacy. Often, this leads to suspicion about ulterior motives. Thus, many critical readings understand "critique" as an uncovering of hidden purposes or latent determinations, frequently in conjunction with philosophical framework theories such as those discussed above. Dan Rowe and Marti Collins, for instance, conduct a rigorous content analysis (of the first season) that questions the show's alliance with Foucauldian concepts of governmentality but not the empirical veracity nor the superior epistemological status of these concepts.[128] In this manner, analytical dislocations can be relocated within prior assessments – and The Wire can be judged ("critically") by its secret deviation from axiomatic norms of dissidence. A ruling figure of thought in this regard describes the show as "complicit" in the very acts of power it condemns. Thus, the series' own practice of social critique, heavily invested in the notion of disembodied authorities working behind the scenes, is applied against itself and surpassed by the explanations of an even more critical observer. Not rarely, this observer concludes that such complicity proves power to be so total that it always incorporates its own critique – a conclusion that actually parallels The Wire's own simultaneous indictment of and aspiration to total vision, as we will see.

It should be noted that such critical readings, despite their reliance on philosophical text models, prove highly perceptive when it comes to identifying the recursive doings of The Wire. They also have an interest in tracing connections between self-descriptions and hetero-descriptions. Sara Taylor looks at HBO's distribution policies, the role of fandom, and "parafilmic material" to disclose "the presence of both reflexivity and compliance to the principles of neoliberalism in The Wire."[129] This perspective, whatever its partisan commitments (particularly to Lisa Duggan's understanding of neoliberalism), enables Taylor to link the show's narrative complexity to its commodity operations: full appreciation of the story requires the purchase of a complete DVD set, etc.

Similarly, a Foucauldian frame allows Ryan Brooks to illustrate how The Wire, despite its insistence on being no cop show, works to produce a powerful notion of "good police" which contrasts the skillful and intuitive labor of individuals with the damage done by judicial checks and balances. In fact, the show's visual and narrative structures establish a "hierarchy of information" which ensures, says Brooks, that the viewers usually know *more* than the gang members and *less* than the police. In other words, a self-propelling series: "there is always more delinquency to uncover." Brooks draws a conclusion that relates the show's inward affiliations (with itself) to its outward affiliations (with its viewers):[130]

> *The Wire* dramatizes the effects of power while simultaneously denying its own power, as a literary entity, to regulate the behavior of its viewers. . . . [T]he show also disavows its own rhetorical strategies by contrasting this rigid discipline with its own authentic knowledge or truth. . . . [T]hese treatments should be understood as part of the narrative power game of *The Wire*, which is an attempt to train viewers to critically question these hierarchies and which, like a police surveillance unit, must remain hidden in order to have its coercive effect.

Other formal analyses are less devoted to detecting "coercive effects." This is not to say that they are disinterested – or should (or even could) be. In fact, they are frequently carried out by television scholars with a keen interest in defining and defending their field of studies. Much argumentative energy is spent on issues of disciplinary identity. In this context, discussions of *The Wire* in terms of its novelistic or literary qualities are likely to be seen as including "a demeaning attitude towards television."[131] A deep investment in the quality of television combined with a necessarily ambivalent attitude toward the concept of Quality TV (when it associates the medium with more esteemed precursors) imparts to these studies a pronounced sense of disciplinary competitiveness. In this fashion, their pervasive concern with televisual complexity and media self-reflexivity parallels the ambiguous strategies of identification and distinction employed by television series themselves. Contemporary media studies of this type even participate in the same processes of competition and one-upmanship so characteristic of their objects, for example by pointing to the material superiority of television over literature or cinema when it comes to telling extensive stories.[132] In fact, of all agents of continuation, American television studies are most directly involved in the formalization, acceleration, and dissemination of *The Wire*'s cultural work.

In terms of analytical intelligence, such proximity can be advantageous. Media scholars and Americanists bring to bear an elaborate historical and formal knowledge on their understanding of *The Wire* – knowledge that is particularly suited, perhaps indispensable, for exploring the cultural movements of an American television series. Whatever their motivations and judgments in terms of disciplinary (and other) identities, these accounts almost inevitably shed light on the narrative's interaction with other narratives, media, and players. For example, *The Wire*'s claims of narrative innovation can be re-contextualized – and made explicit as time-bound ambitions – on a wide field of actors, as in Marsha Kinder's consideration of the show's engagement with movies such as Francesco Rosi's *Salvatore Guiliano*, Sidney Lumet's *Serpico*, Stanley Kubrick's *Paths of Glory* (cited by Simon), Jean-Luc Godard's *Week-End* and, especially, Elia Kazan's *On the Waterfront*, whose divergent representation of dock-workers hints at "the rivalries between movies and television for hyper-realistic representation and systemic analysis, as if the narrative format of cinema is now insufficiently expansive for covering the complex networked society."[133]

Similarly, Jane Gibb and Roger Sabin ask "how new is 'new'?" and suggest "ways in which *The Wire* may be part of a genre tradition" that spans from *Kojak* through *Hill Street Blues*, *Miami Vice*, and *NYPD Blue* all the way to *Homicide*. Unexciting as this claim may appear at first glance, its analytical performance manages to historicize the show's anti-generic self-image and with it the ideas of timeless textuality and reportorial authenticity which play such central roles in scholarship: "[I]n ten, twenty years time," the authors argue, "*The Wire* will look as creaky as those shows appear today." It bears mention that *Dragnet*, the mother of all police procedurals, which today looks like a caricature of television noir, was heralded in the 1950s as the pinnacle of television realism, actually beginning each episode with the line, "Ladies and gentlemen, the story you're about to see is true," followed by a montage of urban locales – an iconographic network – over which the narrator intoned the sentence: "This is the city." Mindful of such (systemic) forebears and transactions, Gibb and Sabin suggest a descriptive approach that is richer in detail and more attuned to the cultural dynamics of its object than sociological duplication, downward identification, activist concern, or upward recognition: "*The Wire* remains the latest in a succession of crime shows that have had a dialogue with each other, as well as with their broader sociological context, and in so doing have allowed America to talk to itself."[134]

Another example of interactional analysis can be found in Jason Mittell's ground-breaking article on *The Wire*'s connection to computer games. Skeptical of Simon's literary comparisons – and hoping instead "to celebrate" *The Wire* "on its own medium's terms" – Mittell phrases his argument in a cautious manner, almost like a thought experiment, but even in such guarded terms it transcends the concerns of disciplinary identity with which it starts. Reminding his readers that "there were many key televised precedents for long-form gradual storytelling for [Simon] to draw upon," Mittell expands this backwards perspective onto present times and charts *The Wire*'s exchanges with its immediate media environment. In so doing, he identifies a crucial arena for contemporary American reality production: "a spectatorial game, being played on-screen for the benefit of an audience."[135]

Thus, the series' creative usage of serial memory – its simultaneous increase and reduction of complexity, in the parlance of the present study – becomes visible as a matter of "ludic joy" and "replayability," i.e., as procedural training that actively involves viewers in the storytelling (and, by implication, in reality construction) even as it seeks to foreclose popular interference. "The show demands audiences to invest in their diegetic memories by rewarding detailed consumption with narrative payoffs," writes Mittell, and as with any productive account, there are a number of ways to proceed from here. Say, by investigating television's commerce with the connectivity of digital competitors or thinking about what it means for cultures when their storytelling media converge around a paradigm of interrelated procedures and short-term tasks for long-term continuations. In either case, analytical dislocation enables perspectives that are particularly responsive to the historical agility of serial narratives.

Examples of this kind of approach are rare.[136] What is more, based on my corpus it seems fair to say that British, Irish, and Australian scholars are more likely than American scholars to challenge the self-images of *The Wire* or set them in dialogue with the series' other involvements.[137] American contributions that do so often subordinate their acts of redescription to an ultimate confirmation of the show's social vision or to proclaiming its status as a masterpiece of television.

So far, only non-American contributions have begun to ask how American writings about *The Wire* relate to the series' cultural activities and conditions. Even so, this is by no means a common question – an indication, perhaps, of the influence of American rehearsals of American Studies over practices in other countries. At the 2009 ESRC conference, according to the paper abstracts, only three presentations (out of fifty) were dedicated to such questions, one of them evidently caught up in a national agenda of its own: David Hesmondhalgh (from the University of Leeds) analyzed how the critical reception of *The Wire* in the United Kingdom "has been marked by a reverence of US production" which is said to go hand in hand with disrespect for British television. Natasha Whiteman (from the University of Leicester) examined how critics and academics "mark their affiliation to the series" through configurations of its quality, comparing such receptions to "modes of identification with media texts evident within online fan communities." Finally and most remarkably, Rebecca Bramall (from the University of Brighton) and Ben Pitcher (from Oxford Brookes University) concluded that *The Wire*'s "appeal to left-wing academics working in the fields of sociology, cultural studies and cognate disciplines" derives from the show's "beguiling projection of sociological desire, providing a totalizing vision of and orientation to the social, a fantasy of the intelligibility of contemporary urban life." According to this reading, *The Wire* resonates with the self-perception of academic practice, defined by its belief in the social value of detailed observation, methodological commitment, and systematic explanation. The show encourages identification among scholars by echoing back to them an "idealized representation" of what they think about themselves.[138]

The fact that the dominant discourses in the United States differ, sometimes dramatically, from such accounts is not a sign of their deficiency or negligence. Rather, it expresses their participation in the cultural doings of the series, i.e., their status as American self-studies. As such, they are open to an American Studies analysis. It can be asked: What are *The Wire* and its readers doing in and for American culture?

3

Habits

The final chapter considers how *The Wire* and its contestations contribute to a larger cultural system which keeps calling itself, not entirely correctly, America. I start from the assumption that "America" is a spacious and imprecise yet efficient and successful term for a geographically vast, socially incongruous, but in no way continentally comprehensive configuration of cultural practices. For this strange, evolving system, mass-produced commercial narratives are crucial agents of continuity. Their performances create unlikely coherence on a daily basis, enabling the culture to achieve and maintain a sense of its own existence and reality through time. Thus, I will read *The Wire* as a serial narrative and a junction of narratives whose cultural work – a work on needs and conflicts of cultural self-definition – makes (and has) a national "home." Consistent with the approach followed so far, I offer these interactions not as the series' true meanings but as perhaps its most lively ones. My aim is to reconstruct effective commonplaces of cultural self-enactment; I call them habits to mark their practical status.

Like almost all stories America has told about itself, *The Wire* stages and engages basic issues of an ongoing national existence. The images, narratives, and debates set in motion by the series coalesce around fundamental questions: (1) What, in America's understanding of itself, constitutes reality? (2) What constitutes society? (3) What constitutes identity? This chapter sketches how *The Wire* is occupied with these questions. I will make brief and broad – altogether more essayistic – propositions for further inquiry.

Hardboiled, Sentimental Nation

In terms of their American performance, the reality effects of *The Wire* are not only a matter of correspondence between some outside world and its televisual representation but also – and perhaps more so – a matter of deep-seated assumptions about what constitutes reality in the United States. At the core of the narrative, perpetuated in its readings and carried over from a large number of precursors, operates a notion of reality that assumes that real life takes place, not in the complacency of secure living, but in a state of exposure, exertion, and incompletion. Entering the stories of *The Wire* mostly through the conduits of naturalistic aesthetics and existentialist (anti)heroism, this belief in the superior reality-status of the hard life is by no means restricted to political dispositions often classified as "liberal," "progressive," or "left-wing" in the United States. It easily reverberates with such currently "right-wing" themes as gun-toting resistance, Tea Party anti-elitism, the fight of ordinary individuals against centralized state institutions, and even the economically liberal belief in the hard factuality of markets, i.e., in the free play of competition, which supposedly rewards assertiveness with success. The shared sense of reality that links all these positions despite their declared opposition permits competing readings of *The Wire*: "socialist" tale for one, obliquely "conservative" parable for another. What remains unchallenged in these interpretive stances are the shared American foundations of such terms – usages often incomprehensible in other parts of the world.

Think about it: Which habits must pertain so that television stories can offer the representation of more violence, and more graphic violence, as signs of enhanced realism? In *The Wire*, too, reality means grittiness. Specifically – and this is where the show takes an identifiable political stand – it means rough living in urban streets, not suburban condos. Moreover, it means urban in a naturalistic sense: the city as jungle, Baltimore, not touristy

Manhattan. A core assumption is that the life of the middle class, anxiously seen as slipping away and yet experienced as constricting at the same time, is somehow less real than the more elemental struggles elsewhere. Insofar as this assumption guides the attitude of HBO subscribers and other viewers, one of the accomplishments of *The Wire* is that it *connects* empirical spaces of consumption to the sense of a reality which constantly proclaims itself absent from them. Everyone from graduate students to the President can now have their favorite drug dealer and benefit from the knowledge and credibility provided by such association. (Barack Obama called Omar his favorite TV character.)[139]

The Wire, in other words, shows a hardboiled world to a culture strongly invested in the higher reality-status of the hardboiled life – quite in the sense in which Walter Mosley defines the term "hardboiled" as referring to a situation "when the hammer is coming down and there's not a friend you can count on."[140] What is more, the series understands itself as a hardboiled laborer in the drama of American social life. In the words of one of its writers, talking about his research for the show, "We heard about men who could steal the devil's pitchfork, others who could drink all night and work all day."[141] David Simon's sporadic preference for rhetorical flourishes reminiscent of George W. Bush – "Make no mistake" – is no coincidence in this regard.[142] Such determination accords with Simon's complaint, voiced in a DVD feature for Season Three, that New York City by now has more homicides on television than in real life, as if this would diminish the city's reality, whereas Baltimore is the true capital of physical violence, as if this would enhance its authenticity.[143] In the same manner, viewers can identify themselves in blog entries as coming from "Bodymore, Murdaland" (a graffiti shown in the title sequence of Season One). Conversely, but following the same logic, Charles Dutton, the African American director of *The Corner*, questions Simon's credentials to even talk about these things, because there is always an even deeper knowledge of harsh reality:

> David Simon can visit and sit with as many black folks in this
> city as he wants to. . . . They can pay the families to get the
> stories. They can listen and walk around with dopefiends.
> They can write about murders, and they still won't know a
> damn thing about black people. . . . I know what it feels like
> to kill somebody. I know what it feels like to get shot. I know
> what it feels like that people be looking to kill me. I don't have
> to show up as a crime journalist after the fact.[144]

Obviously, Dutton's notion of genuine knowledge ("what it feels
like to kill somebody") is deeply intertwined with forceful claims
of group distinction ("to know about black people"). But
regardless which concrete vision of belonging is asserted here,
its structural similarity to other American tales of authenticity
suggests that the hardboiled definition of reality organizes
competing claims to American realism. In this sense, the stories
of endangerment, oppression, and survival told by and through
The Wire may mutally surpass and supersede each other, but this
very competition stabilizes their joint national range. In the
words of Mosley, "From our prisons to our ghettos, from our
boardrooms to the Oval Office, from gangsta rap to the Patriot
Act, America is a hardboiled nation."[145]

If being real means knowledge of struggle, *The Wire* must be
haunted by its own (social, economic, media, geographic)
distance from the world it talks about. It is this anxiety, above all,
which animates the show's enactment of insider information. In
his interview with Nick Hornby, Simon confesses that he was
afraid someone more knowing might come along and call it all a
bluff. By all means to be avoided was the impression of being
"lamely white and unnuanced."[146] In conjunction with the series'
encouragement of downward identification, this is not simply a
concern about doing journalism properly. Rather, *The Wire* is

apprehensive of its standing with the very people it evidently feels and fears it objectifies. Hence Simon's pervasive self-fashioning as the streetwise pariah, the man who's seen it all and is respected for it among the natives. In more conventional terms, Brett Martin's *Difficult Men* feeds into the same narrative – not only in its sections on Simon – when it describes television's contemporary innovators as if they were characters in their own shows. In fact, there has been since the 19th century a pronounced current in American cultural production that is characterized by its desire to operate outside the mainstream *because* such position entails the possibility of being accepted *by* those with more credible – and usually less voluntary – claims to be outsiders.[147] Popular culture, in particular, has reproduced and nourished this desire, and with it the habit of thinking of America as situated away from the habitats of its elite, intellectual, feminized, Europeanized, or money-grabbing occupants: a true nation somewhere out there – an expansive reality in the unfinished open, simultaneously thought of as physical victim and hidden home of national practices. It may be useful to discuss *The Wire* as performing in this American tradition of organizing national spaces as near or distant, phony or real.

Of course, it is a small step from the hardboiled to the senti-mental, as any reader of Ernest Hemingway or Sarah Palin knows. Amanda Klein has argued that *The Wire* shares with conventional Western melodrama "a focus on powerless victims, an emphasis on corruption and injustice as the primary source of conflict, and the characters' frustrating inability to effect change around them" – tactics which since *Oliver Twist* and *Uncle Tom's Cabin*, not to mention *Capital*, have functioned "to place the weak on a higher moral plane than the powerful."[148] For obvious reasons, revolutionary, democratic, and post-colonial societies are especially habituated to such assumptions. The United States is all three things, and here the notion that power is fundamen-tally oppressive and that being threatened or victimized bestows virtue appears so self-evident that it offers rival self-descriptions for the entire spectrum of popular politics. (Even the most conservative patriotism typically presents itself as resisting powerful oppressors, and elites can rarely afford to appear as such.)[149] *The Wire* plays its part, and a vigorous one, rendering more likely the nation's unlikely belief in its continuity by telling hardboiled, sentimental – "gritty," viewers say, and "heart-breaking" – stories about the likes of Dukie, Cutty, and Bubbles, themselves continuations of "achingly human characters" from centuries of American storytelling about America.[150] Perhaps no other culture has done more – literally, in the sense of energies spent and money paid – to create, for characters and with them, a sense of its own spacious humanity.

Visibility and Commitment

The Wire's hardboiled sentimentalism is also in evidence when the show sentimentalizes itself as a neglected outcast program, snubbed by the Emmy machinery and marginalized by competitors more mainstream and more powerful than itself: facts that make it possible to transpose onto the series its own project of rendering visible an unseen reality. Surely, to frame the visible as invisibility undone is a key praxis of *The Wire* and perhaps of American popular culture at large. "The artifice of television . . . made it real for millions who'd never seen anything like it," explains a writer for the show, calling to mind the original meaning of the term tele-vision: viewing what is far away.[151] A crucial function of American television, Mittell notes, has always been to "represent aspects of the world unfamiliar to typical viewers."[152] In this regard, American television has always operated as a news medium, even in its narrative genres. As Robyn Warhol argues, the serialized structure of these genres inevitably picks up on sequential real-life events, which are in turn experienced as serial narratives by becoming daily news.[153] In this manner, television not only structures time schedules from one end of the continent to the other, but also organizes – as the inventors of the "extended republic" would not be surprised to learn – dissimilar and simultaneous realities into recurring patterns of narrative renewal.[154] The challenge is to do so repeatedly and in the process incorporate ever more reality into the nation's ongoing demonstration of itself. America's story is both expansive and binding, by definition. *The Wire*, too, continues a project of republican tele-visuality that ranges from *Amos 'n' Andy* (providing "opportunities for visibility and employment for black actors") to *Good Times* and beyond, offering one more "look at a facet of American culture that had been previously ignored by television."[155]

These considerations shed some light on *The Wire*'s theory of society. To begin with, social existence, according to the show, is crucially dependent on the condition of *being seen* by others. The link of visibility and social life informs especially the series' economic narrative. At first glance, this narrative talks about the essential similarity of crime and business – a critical redescription that has been read as underlining the show's systemic social vision but that most of all might hearken back to earlier popular texts such as *The Godfather*.[156] Season One, in particular, draws repeated parallels between legitimate and illegitimate types of labor, trade, and investment. The unsettling implication is that lawful commerce is naturally close to crime. In later seasons, however, it becomes clear that the two spheres, despite their structural resemblance, are quite distinct. No substitution seems possible. Characters who want to run the underground economy like legitimate business inevitably fail. Stringer Bell is not saved by taking courses in micro-economics or studying *Robert's Rules of Order*. Conversely, when Bunny Colvin tries to legitimize the drug economy within a free trade safety zone, this capitalist move minimizes crime and murder for a while, as Adam Smith would have predicted, but Colvin's scheme and his career stand no chance of survival.

With regard to economics, then, *The Wire* tells a tale of two, or perhaps, of many, cities. We see a world of parallel societies mutually inaccessible and often invisible to each other. Culture trumps economy. A favorite scenario shows respected players in one social sphere acting like inexperienced fools in another. Stringer Bell is conned by a senator because he does not understand the rules of politics. When fearsome Marlo tries to withdraw money from his bank account, he is reduced to helpless anger because he does not comprehend how banks operate. When Colvin takes a group of crafty street kids to a fancy restaurant, they panic, supposedly because they do not know what to do with the cutlery – suggesting that they have never watched television.

Clearly, the society constructed by *The Wire* suffers from lack of practical integration. The show's resulting advocacy of inclusiveness is particularly conspicuous in seasons Two and Four, about "the death of work" and the educational system, respectively.[157] Here, the series deplores, not the crypto-criminal structure of capitalist trade (except in its international form), but that American capitalism does not provide enough room for all its members. The school episodes suggest that kids who become drug dealers do so because the official economy has no need for them. In interviews, Simon calls this a "post-industrial" condition. What he means is not so much that technological and service-sector innovations have diminished the demand for manual labor, but that globalized forces – think of the Greek, who is not even Greek! – drain the nation of its integrative capacities:

> Listen, capitalism is the only engine credible enough to generate mass wealth. I think it's imperfect, but we're stuck with it. And thank God we have that in the toolbox. But if you don't manage it in some way that you incorporate all of society ... if you don't have a sense of shared purpose,

national purpose, then all it is a pyramid scheme [*sic*]. . . . I feel that the republic is actually in danger. . . . I mean it would be one thing with an oligarchy and they were doing a better job of it. I would be okay with that. . . . This is how an empire is eaten from within.[158]

In full keeping with these pronouncements, the show's economic ideal is one in which the nation would *contain* capitalism. Like in Franklin D. Roosevelt's Fireside Chats, the nation should have an economy, not be run by one – which always implies: not be run by interests foreign to its shores.[159] In quite this sense, Alberto Toscano and Jeff Kinkle have diagnosed the series' "ideological position" (meaning its most energetic economic assumption) as "a kind of labourist social critique, infused by a dose of nostalgia for the Fordist compact" that has a lot in common "with a nostalgic valorisation of the moral economy of work and craft (present, for instance, in the influential works of Richard Sennett)" and that "bears a kinship – albeit in the mode of bitter mourning – with the 'labouring of American culture' studied by Michael Denning."[160]

Nostalgia for the moral economy of work and craft is the important point; it goes a long way toward elucidating what *The Wire* is doing with – and within – the question of American society. In fact, all seasons are about work-places and their decline: good police work is harder and harder to do, labor unions have been ruined, true journalists are a dying breed, etc. Everything was better when it was done manually by dedicated individuals: an American jeremiad of vocation.[161] The show's social vision is largely dominated by a philosophy of honest, if often futile work: a populist ethos of rule-bending resilience infused with existentialist charisma.[162] Simon explains that in all his television narratives "there exists, I believe, an abiding faith in the capacity of individuals, a careful acknowledgment of our possibilities, our humor and wit, our ability to somehow endure."[163] An entire lexicon of American self-definitions is assembled in this short profile: existence, belief, abiding, faith, capacity, individuals, possibilities, ability, endure, our. Similarly, Barack Obama likes to talk about the "fundamental decency" of ordinary Americans trying to make ends meet.

Thus, the misery of parallel societies, parallel invisibilities, is redeemed – and this is not too strong a word for these small acts of perseverance – by what can be seen in all of them: the value of commitment, the belief in the inherent righteousness of a job well done. The heroes – and there are many in *The Wire* under an existentialist definition of the term – are those who are committed against all odds: to traditional police work like Bunk and McNulty, to systematic observation like Lester Freamon, to teaching like Pryzbylewski, to some personal code like Omar. If we resent a character, Simon says, or change our attitude toward him, it is because of the character's "unwillingness to commit."[164]

Significantly, commitment is also what *The Wire* demands from its viewers. The economy of hard work and fair reward rules not only the series' narrative but also its narration. "We were making the drama," Simon underlines, "for those [who] devote enough effort . . . those who gave it their all." The labor-requirements of serial complexity (concentration, patience, reflection, etc.), emphasized here no less fully than in television scholarship, correspond to the work ethic promoted in and by the story: "the reward for . . . committed viewers," explains Simon, "would come not at the end of a scene or the end of an episode, but at the end of the season, indeed, at the end of the tale." As far as "storytelling" goes, this "seemed like the best way to do business."[165] In this context, it seems useful to think of HBO's much-touted policy of "rewatchability" (where the payoff comes not necessarily in the end but through unwavering loyalty until the end) as an imperative of *attention*, competing for that scarcest of resources in an age of digital connectivity.

At the same time, *The Wire* is committed to its own project of social visibility. The Fordist ideal of national capitalism channels serial proliferations into what one critic called a "sprawling portraiture that aims at inclusivity."[166] The result, paradoxically, is a panorama of fragmentation: a totalizing vision of reciprocal invisibilities. Put differently: unlike other HBO series – in fact, unlike most series that follow the cultural forum model of American television – *The Wire* often wants to show itself as "driven by a coherent worldview."[167] If serial complexity is dependent on a self-organizing system of continual reductions, *The Wire*'s efforts to control its own (ideological) expansiveness are an almost perfect example of such dialectics. This also clarifies why the show has no interest in including itself among its players (as long-running serial narratives frequently do), for this would threaten its performances of an all-encompassing, finalizing perspective.

The "rewards" of such a perspective, as Simon says, should come in the end – but even before, their power to inspire devotion is immense, as could be seen in Chapter Two. The finale is just particularly true to the series' comforting organization of discomforting realities. In the end, we get closure without exit. The story suggests its own prolongation by fully confirming itself. Things fall into place by continuing their narrative run: Haynes recognizes Templeton for who he is; Templeton's moral failure is all the more apparent for his public success and bright future; Freamon follows the trail of money, even though neither Marlo nor Levy will be prosecuted, but the police work was good, and Marlo returns to the streets that, we know somehow, will kill him; McNulty can leave smirking, prematurely eulogized as "the best we had"; the game goes on with different people but Bubbles has his heroic media moment, Michael outwits Marlo, Cheese is shot, and Proposition Joe is revenged. The narrative sees it all, far into the future, no screen goes blank, and no television set looks as if it has short-circuited itself.

It finally becomes clear why *The Wire* is so amenable to Foucauldian readings, especially in the Anglo-American version of Foucault's (earlier and more famous) texts. Both types of narrative understand power to be essentially restrictive – notwithstanding qualifications in Foucault's later work – and liberation to be inherently righteous. Both claim to address invisible but omnipresent structures. Both, in doing so, engage in totalizing supervisions. They tell *powerful* stories, stories of finalization. Making visible how identities are made, they make identities (of reading, thinking, writing). Faced with these observations, we are not forced to perpetuate the game of mutually superseding critiques by turning *The Wire* or *Discipline and Punish* into ideologically unified accomplices of the power they conjure and condemn. Instead, it is possible to ask how the unlikely authority of these texts – replete as they are with other stories, genres, and actors, many from long ago and far away – comes into existence and which services they fulfill.

Finding Oneself on Television

When readers of serial narratives publicly mourn the death of their favorite character or write in to the author(s) to inquire about a character's untold past and future, this is not because they confuse reality and story, says Jared Gardner, but because they understand that they have a role to play.[168] It is a role offered and required by the feedback economy of ongoing popular storytelling: an identity that gains reality through its presence in public stories. For early newspaper readers, Gardner argues, serial comics became like daily news about their own lives: narratives of recognition that worked well because they were not about "real people one cannot see" but about "fictional people one can see."[169] To be seen means to be real, especially in a nation of states united. Obviously, any aesthetic of immersion strives for experiences that appear to be more immediate than non-narrative reality itself. Less obvious are the transactions between these imperceptible mediations and American notions of identity. One thing seems certain: Realistic storytelling invites people not only to lose themselves in the story but also – perhaps even more so – to find themselves there.[170]

As we saw, characters of *The Wire* will not stay contained within their story-world. In a remarkably wide sample of instances, viewers and commentators have detected them in real life, and this, in turn, has encouraged actual people to speak (and perhaps think) of themselves as *Wire* characters. The volume *Truth Be Told* features chapters in which the real-life inspirations for leading figures are compared not only with their fictional representations but with the actors playing these characters. In the same spirit, Reverend Eugene F. Rivers led a study group at Harvard, which used *The Wire* to examine, among other things, "what the life of the young drug dealer Bodie" – clearly approached as a person here – "can tell us about" the differences between structural and cultural causes of black poverty. The group invited Michael Williams, the actor who played Omar, to discuss, not his personal opinions, but "how his character would have interpreted the meaning of the Obama presidency."[171]

On the one hand, one can think of such developments as variations of the *CSI* effect ("where juries expect more conclusive revelations from forensic evidence than are possible based on the assumptions fostered by the hit crime franchise").[172] With Farhad Manjoo, one might even attribute them to a "post-fact society," in which internet rumors and fake autobiographies have replaced reliable information.[173] On the other hand, *The Wire* is committed exactly to such disappearing notions of reliability, and Rivers no doubt knows that Michael Williams is not Omar. More important, therefore, than the narratological blunder of these practices (collapsing the difference between character and person) is their everyday productivity, particularly in terms of performing identity in contemporary America.

It should be remembered that *The Wire* provides self-confirmation for an impressive variety of viewers. Not only is the show able to report a group's worldview back to it as factual information and authentic emotion, it even and explicitly seeks to provoke such scenes of recognition. "I want," says Simon,

> a homicide detective, or a drug slinger, or a longshoreman, or a politician anywhere in America to sit up and say, Whoa, that's how my day is. That's my goal. . . . [W]hat I wanted was that longshoremen across America would watch *The Wire* and say, Cool, they know my world. I've never seen my world depicted on TV, and these guys got it.[174]

Simon got his wish. A standard situation in the reception of *The Wire* is people finding themselves in the show. In fact, such scenes of recognition are an important part of the marketing of the series; incorporated in the show's paratexts, they become part of its wider narrative in DVD specials or publications like *Truth Be Told*, where real people call it all real and are displayed as doing so. In other words, the show's realism has its own narrative, folded back into its self-description and opening up different spaces for audience reciprocation.

More often than not, these responses reinforce the hardboiled creed of visibility and commitment that drives the television narrative itself. Alvarez, quoting a police reporter from St. Louis, makes clear that being a good crime reporter is not about "fancy back rooms where deals are made or soirees at the country club," but about visiting "really crappy areas": "Covering crime takes you to these places . . . in all their fucked-up grandeur." Is it surprising that the man who has worked in such places carries on a narrative that shows him doing so heroically? Under which circumstances could it be different? "I liked [this work] because it was real," he declares in a book bent on establishing the gritty realism of precisely such statements.[175]

Thus, to read the endorsements of cops, reporters, gang

members, etc. as part of *The Wire*'s cultural work is to ask how *The Wire* – and with it the lively genre of American crime television – contributes to the public demeanor and indeed the labor practices of cops, reporters, gang members, etc. The fact that such endorsements are often accompanied by expressions of gratitude corresponds with the show's belief that respect requires, first and foremost, visibility: "I've never seen my world depicted on TV," Simon ventriloquizes his subjects. If we turn this statement upside down, we put it on its feet: Seeing something on TV, it can become my world. If you are not represented, you have no identity.

The way American viewers have related to *The Wire* bears this out: The show's interest in stable and ultimately unbridgeable spheres of belonging, with a heroic undercurrent of free-floating individuals and honest workers in all fields, is echoed by competing readings which publicly align themselves with this or that identity displayed. What they have in common is summarized by Afaa Weaver, who uses the show as a backdrop for his personal memoirs: "I long for home."[176]

Consider how American television has always been busy helping the citizens of an implausibly extended republic to come home, but this again and again, hence paradoxically, because few homes in this nation exist without effort. Many efforts, however, have become habitual. Thus, when George Pelecanos, writer for *The Wire*, says that his "mission" is "to illuminate and dignify . . . lives to a public that rarely reads about them or recognizes their humanity in film, television, and fiction," the assumption is that dignity and humanity do indeed presuppose an audience – ideally one that sees you acting in national stories.[177] In this context, Schaub's comparison between *The Wire* and reality TV takes on a wider meaning, because even beyond its casting policies does the series create "possibilities for ordinary people . . . to have leading roles."[178] Pelecanos thinks that these possibilities feed directly into the lives and identities of the people involved: "At best," he writes, "a viewer might watch our show and be inspired to become the kind of extraordinary person . . . that I can only conjure up as a fictional character in my head."[179] The humility of the word "only" is misleading; so is the less humble belief that such conjuring – or "inspiration" – is the act of merely one head. In fact, Pelecanos's scenario expresses a long-standing project of national reproduction: The way to improve American society is to make (good) characters.

Republican education means to watch oneself being represented, except that it does not always work this way. Not all viewers have relished such casting opportunities. When Mark Bowden interviewed David Simon, he noted with some irritation that "I could see myself morphing into a character in his show."[180] Overall, however, there is something suitably modern, and something curiously American, about writing autobiography with public material. Such resources almost inevitably turn the question of identity into a function of professed collective belonging. The American type of culture may have accepted earlier than others that personal identity is performed in the eyes of others – rather than something that people carry inside themselves – but being aware of an audience burdens the practice of being oneself with considerable problems of representation and performance. There are the questions of association, opportunity, and recognition: Who do I relate to? Where and when? Who sees me acting in this way? How will I be appreciated for it? Apparently, performed belongings are no less demanding – and in the end, no less normative – than essentialist ones. They may not haunt a person in the same way as the idea of blood ties can, but they formulate an ever-present imperative to "have" an identity. There is no opting out of the game of collective interpersonal differentiation – and again, *The Wire* and its American readers are a case in point. Everything that makes American culture in the age of empire anxiety and empire denial is here: the demand to know who you are and to profess it repeatedly by means of public, often commercial and serialized material, the ever-deeper intertwining of subjective experience and assertive home(land) claims, the spatial and mental clustering of like-minded individuals away from suspected mainstreams of centralized power, individualism's need for continual communal expression, the valuation of community over society, incongruously mixed up with nostalgia for some kind of unified national purpose. *The Wire* does its work on and within these habits.

Notes

1   Weisberg, "The Wire on Fire." Almost simultaneously, Lowry wrote in *Variety:* "When television history is written, little else will rival *The Wire*, a series of such extraordinary depth and ambition that it is, perhaps inevitably, savored only by an appreciative few" ("The Wire").

2   How often do we advise a colleague or are told by one: "You should publish this, before someone else does"? The implications for academic knowledge production are interesting. For the present study, I have surveyed a sample of approximately 200 publications from newspapers, internet sources, and academic venues, compiled with the help of Anne Clausen, to whom I wish to express my gratitude. The bulk of these contributions appeared between 2006 and 2010, with a significant academic reception starting in 2008. The contributions in Liam Kennedy and Stephen Shapiro's volume *The Wire: Race, Class, and Genre* (2012), in which a shorter version of Chapter Two appeared, are not part of my corpus.

3   See Latour, *Reassembling the Social,* especially 43-50, 213-18 (including following quotations).

4   This project differs from ANT-inspired readings that investigate the representation of networks or non-human actors in fictional texts. In a typical scene of theoretical self-recognition, such readings often treat their narratives as allegories of ANT itself. Compare Jagoda on *The Wire:* "the series operates as an aesthetically rich counterpart to actor-network-theory" ("Wired," 193). For the coinage work-net, see Latour, *Reassembling,* 132.

5   See, especially, Luhmann, *Die Gesellschaft der Gesellschaft.*

6   Such philosophical reserve may even be in accordance with Actor-Network-Theory itself, because more than any other

master-theory on offer, ANT has been struggling hard to shed its master-theoretical ambitions, promising to move us from Theory to methodology, from charismatic thought to actual work. For the term "sensitizing concept," see Blumer, *Symbolic Interactionism*.

7 See Kelleter, "Toto, I think we're in Oz again." Many of the themes discussed in the following have been developed in the Research Unit "Popular Seriality – Aesthetics and Practice," funded by the German Research Foundation (DFG); compare Kelleter, *Populäre Serialität*; Mayer, *Serial Fu Manchu*. On serial authorship, see Kelleter and Stein, "Autorisierungspraktiken seriellen Erzählens."

8 My interest in self-description is obviously indebted to Luhmann's understanding of the term, although this study treats self-descriptions not under theoretical but pragmatic considerations; see Luhmann, *Gesellschaft*, 879-93. Just as in the case of ANT, no rigorous attempt will be made to secure system theory's own systemic coherence. The complementary term to "Selbstbeschreibung" (self-description) in Luhmann's model is "Fremdbeschreibung." There is no good English translation for this term; hence, Chapter Two resorts to the slightly awkward coinage "hetero-description."

9 This is especially true for long-running narratives that may be older than their contemporary human actors (the term "actor" here referring to any force involved in a series' continuation). New writers have to perform their authorship against the limiting background of established roles and rules within the narrative (e.g., what are a hero's powers, which character traits are possible, etc.) and often in competition with established ownership claims outside the narrative (see Bob Kane's jealous guardianship of the original Batman character); long-term readers can challenge innovations with an authoritative appeal to "continuity"

(notice the effect of the *Comic Book Price Guide*, first published in 1970, on superhero storytelling). For these and additional examples, see Kelleter and Stein, "Autorisierungspraktiken." *The Wire* does not follow the format of the open-ended series frequent in comics, but the disruption of text/paratext distinctions is also visible in "serials" with progressing story-arcs. In general it can be said that the difference between a series and a serial, well established in Anglo-American media studies since Raymond Williams's *Television*, is less clear-cut than suggested even by the usual heuristic disclaimers.

10 Simon, "Introduction," 10-11. *Truth Be Told* features the HBO logo on its title page, is copyrighted (though not published) by Home Box Office, Inc., and can be bought alongside other *Wire* paraphernalia in HBO's boutique store in New York City.

11 For the "audience exchange" within the traditional network economy, see Mittell, *Television and American Culture*, 54-98.

12 For the cultural forum model, see Newcomb and Hirsch, "Television as Cultural Forum." Of course, even on cable a show's popularity often depends on providing a wide spectrum of possible identifications (see *The Sopranos* or *Six Feet Under*).

13 In the late 1990s and early 2000s, before the serial successes of other subscription channels like AMC, a number of academic studies took up and perpetuated this focus on HBO; among the first were Edgerton and Jones, *Essential HBO Reader*, and Leverette et al., *It's Not TV*. For earlier Quality TV discourses, see Feuer et al., *MTM*; Thompson, *Television's Second Golden Age*.

14 See Jahn-Sudmann and Kelleter, "Dynamik serieller Überbietung." We define serial one-upmanship or outbidding (*Überbietung*) as the repeated intensification of successfully established levels of inter-serial and intra-serial distinction.

(The term "intra-serial" describes a series' competitive relation to itself, the term "inter-serial" its competitive relation to other series. Both types of serial competition, we argue, support the historical self-observation of serial formats, i.e., their meta-serial intelligence.)

15 Simon, "Introduction," 1. The following quote ibid. 16-17.

16 See Kelleter, "Populärkultur und Kanonisierung."

17 O'Rourke, "Behind the Wire."

18 Talbot, "Stealing Life." On Shakespeare and *The Wire*, see Hornby, "David Simon"; Scott, "Who Gets to Tell a Black Story?"

19 King, "Exclusive David Simon Q & A."

20 By far the most prominent key term in the reception and self-presentation of *The Wire* is "reality." At one point of this project, I planned to take stock of the various meanings of this term and its derivatives in interviews, articles, documentaries, etc., but quickly gave up.

21 On the link between on-location shooting and a sense of televisual quality, see Perren, "I Don't Think We're in Hollywood Anymore." Compare David Simon: "none of us is from Hollywood . . . we are not even from the literary capital of New York" ("Introduction," 10).

22 Simon, "Letter to HBO," 33.

23 Mittell, "The Television Context."

24 Compare Simon in Sodano: "Secretly, we all know we get more ink for being shut out. So at this point, we *wanna* be shut out" ("Critic-Adored, Awared-Ignored"). Instead of winning an Emmy, Simon received a McArthur genius grant.

25 Hornby, "David."

26 Hornby, "David"; Weisberg, "Wire." For "televised novel," see Lanahan, "Secrets of the City," 24.

27 The pioneering discussion of *The Wire* outside the novel-paradigm is Mittell, "All in the Game," one of the first bona

fide scholarly works on the series. For TV studies on *The Wire*, see the section "Analytical Dislocation" in Chapter Two below.

28 Burkeman, "Arrogant? Moi?"

29 Wolfe, "New Journalism," 55. For the term "parajournalism," see Wolfe 45. The phrase "the way we live now" is Trollope's and ranks among Wolfe's favorite quotations to define his subject matter. There are obvious echoes of Wolfe in Simon's summation of what *The Wire* is about: "the drug war. Or politics. Or race. Or education, labor relations or journalism. It was about The City. It is how we in the West live at the millennium" ("Introduction," 3). Linda Williams also mentions Wolfe as an influence on Simon ("Ethnographic Imaginary," 215).

30 Wolfe, "New," 36, 22, 37, 27.

31 Simon's *Homicide: A Year on the Killing Streets*, about the Baltimore Police Department, was published in 1991. *The Corner: A Year of an Inner-City Neighborhood*, about community life and the drug trade in West Baltimore, co-authored with former detective Ed Burns (co-producer and writer for *The Wire*), appeared in 1997. *Homicide* was turned into a police procedural by NBC (1993-1999), with Simon working on the writing staff; HBO transformed *The Corner*, with Simon as a writer, into a mini-series in 2000. *The Wire* was the first of Simon's Baltimore narratives to be written and produced directly for television without previous book publication. However, Bowden (in "The Angriest Man in Television") has pointed to *The Wire*'s affinity to non-fiction novels such as Truman Capote's *In Cold Blood* (1966), Tom Wolfe's *The Right Stuff* (1979), and Norman Mailer's *The Executioner's Song* (1980). On Simon's books and their importance for *The Wire*, see especially Williams, "Ethnographic."

32 For the influence of naturalism, see also Tyree, "The Wire,"

36; Aiello, "Politics, Postmodernism, and the Rebirth of American Naturalism"; Bieger, "It's All in the Game."

33 Moyers, "Simon on Fact and Fiction."

34 See Williams: "Fans of *The Wire* will recognize in [Simon's] op-ed rants many of the crucial themes of the series, as well as the genesis for many of its greatest dramatic actions. . . . In the ethnographic journalism of *Homicide* and *The Corner*, the op-ed comes alive and ceases to be an angry white man's rant. We are relieved of Simon's most impassioned prose because it has been rendered as drama, arising from the mouth of characters" ("Ethnographic," 224).

35 "The story is labeled as fiction, which is to say we took liberties in a way that journalism cannot and should not do" (Simon, "Introduction," 29).

36 Mittell, "All," 435. See also: "*The Wire* avoids flashbacks, voice-over, fantasy sequences, repetition from multiple perspectives, or reflexive commentaries on the narrative form itself" (ibid.).

37 Wolfe, "New," 35. The quotation in the next paragraph ibid. 48.

38 Bowden even detects a "desire to show people how wrong they are" ("Angriest").

39 See Williams, "Ethnographic," especially 210-215.

40 Wolfe, "New," 18.

41 Ibid. 49; Alvarez, *Truth*, 64; "ESRC Conference Outline."

42 Bowden, "Angriest."

43 Kois and Sternbergh, "Debating the Legacy of 'The Wire'."

44 Simon, "Introduction," 3.

45 The term "complexity" is particularly suitable for claims of *Überbietung*, especially when it is used as a comparative that engenders further comparatives: "Here again, *The Wire* exhibits more narrative complexity than most other series-serial hybrids," writes Nannicelli, because it "embraces seriality to such a great degree" and "track[s] more narrative

threads that reemerge sporadically and circuitously over greater periods of time" ("It's All Connected," 18). The series' claim to unsurpassed obscenity is memorably performed in a famous scene in episode 1.4, where McNulty and Bunk investigate a crime scene, their three-minute dialogue consisting of only one word ("fuck") persistently repeated in various inflections and derivatives.

46 For a discussion of series as "vast narratives," see Harrigan and Wardrip-Fruin, *Third Person*. The best discussion of narrative complexity in American television is one of the first: Mittell, "Narrative Complexity."

47 Simon, "Introduction," 20.

48 Simon in Talbot, "Stealing." The term "multisited ethnography" is used by Williams to align Simon's brand of journalism with George Marcus's *Ethnography through Thick and Thin* ("Ethnographic"). On *Lost*, see Kelleter, "Whatever Happened, Happened."

49 See Hayward, *Consuming Pleasures*; Kelleter, "Populäre Serialität."

50 See Kelleter, "Toto"; Mayer, *Serial*. Here as elsewhere, I use the adjective "serial" as a general term for all types of commercial seriality, not just narratives extending story arcs over many episodes, as in the series/serial-dichotomy common in Anglo-American media studies. My own distinction between series and oeuvres makes such "serials" into a sub-type of the first category (whereas so-called "mini-series" – pre-established structures with a limited number of episodes usually produced en bloc prior to their initial reception – fall under the category of oeuvre or work).

51 The sentence is also quoted at the top of page 1 of *Truth Be Told*. Altogether, it is one of the most frequently cited pieces of dialogue from the series in the scholarly literature and hence one of its most influential self-descriptions.

52 "We assume that all main events presented in the narrative are related to one another in a chain of causality" (Mittell, *Television*, 217).

53 Simon, "I meant this, not that."

54 This is not to deny that Simon made a serious political point when he insisted that this was not the important question to ask. But Bill Simmons's question has been produced by the series' own acts of storytelling. David Simon's position must not be confused here with the actor-network to which it contributes.

55 King, "Exclusive."

56 Alvarez, *Truth*, 96. See also Michael Williams, the actor who played Omar: "They were thinking of killing off Omar in the first season but didn't. And they made sure that none of the directors ever tried to tweak Omar" (ibid. 316). Simon's statement that he pays no attention to audience reactions is taken from an interview on a fan website for *The Wire*. The interview ends with Simon thanking Jim King "for maintaining the Yahoo group and Homicide: Links on the Sites." The quotation above is followed by Simon's quali-fying remark: "We do look online to get a general sense of viewers' reaction and whether or not our themes are getting through or whether we need to explain ourselves a little better, or perhaps, a little less" (King, "Exclusive"). Note that Simon's rejection of feedback ("not at all open to suggestions") is based on a strong sense of control over which influences are active in his narrative decisions.

57 Compare Zborowski, "The Rhetoric of *The Wire*."

58 Simon in Ryan, "David Simon Talks." These conventional television strategies of representing individuality conflict with the show's "systemic" readings (most prominently in Chaddha and Wilson, "Way Down in the Hole") but also with "network" interpretations (like Jagoda, "Wired"), which overestimate the originality of a TV series not having

a central protagonist.

59 In an early analysis, Dignan takes this as a mark of *The Wire*'s artistic uniqueness. The way he phrases it, however, sounds like popular seriality pure and simple: "[Characters] become different people. They've taken promotions or moved into completely different professions; they've sparked up new relationships and abandoned old ones that have run their course. Like its characters, *The Wire* evolves, moving beyond themes it has already explored and letting itself veer into new territory."

60 For series as "cumulative narratives," see Newcomb, "Magnum, P.I." Also compare Kraniauskas, "Elasticity of Demand," 26.

61 See Simon in Talbot, "Stealing."

62 Alvarez, *Truth*, 281.

63 See Havrilesky, "David Simon on Cutting 'The Wire'"; Tucker, "High 'Wire'." Sternbergh sums it up: "For everyone who felt cheated by the stubbornly ambivalent series finale of *The Sopranos* – which is to say, everyone – there can be no such complaints about *The Wire*" ("The Anti-'Sopranos'").

64 See Kelleter, "Populärkultur." Similarly Jahn-Sudmann and Starre, "Experimente des Quality TV."

65 Sternbergh, "Anti"; Tucker, "High."

66 Simon, "Introduction," 3. He continues: "To the greatest possible extent, we were quick to renounce the theme" (ibid.). Diametrically opposed to Simon's reading of the show, we find viewers like Williams, whose investment in the (moral and epistemological) value of melodrama has her claim that efficient storytelling is all but inconceivable without such contrasts: To cast "nuance and complexity versus the melodramatic black-and-white worldview," she argues, "would be to succumb to the simplified vilification of melodrama itself as precisely the story of good and evil

that Simon claims to have renounced but cannot renounce if he is to tell a compelling serial story" ("Ethnographic," 221).

67 Kraniauskas, "Elasticity," 27.

68 Compare Jahn-Sudmann: "An essential function of any series consists in reducing self-generated complexities or organizing them in such a manner that they are narratively clear and comprehensible" ("Serienzeit und serielle Zeitlichkeit," my translation).

69 It is a problem of a different order to ask how discourses of American TV reverberate in other countries. This question can be ignored in the present context because scholarly activities in non-English-speaking countries are largely irrelevant for research practices in the United States. In the US, the field of American Studies is only rarely compelled to imagine itself open to competent outside descriptions, especially if they are phrased in foreign languages. The field tends to conceive of American Studies outside the US, not as offering the possibility of epistemologically advantaged redescriptions, but, if at all, as part of its own transnational diversity (see Kelleter, "Transnationalism"). For a brief discussion of English-language publications from academic cultures outside the US, see this chapter's final section.

70 Anderson, "No Such Thing as Good and Evil"; Ethridge, "Baltimore on *The Wire*," 155 (Ethridge makes direct reference to Simon); Lanahan, "Secrets," 24.

71 E.g., "*The Wire* presents a complex and nuanced portrait of American urban culture that transcends cynicism with a faith in the complexity of people and circumstances" (Beliveau and Bolf-Beliveau, "Posing Problems and Picking Fights," 102).

72 Beliveau and Bolf-Beliveau, "Posing"; Clandfield, "We ain't got no yard"; Peterson, "Corner-Boy Masculinity"; Suderman, "Tension City"; Read, "Stringer Bell's Lament," 124; Blundell, "Social Justice"; Jagoda, "Wired," 193;

"ESRC." The show can also disprove positions: Sidhu uses it as "an element of practical reality" that "challenges" the constitutional theories of Charles Posner ("Wartime America").

73 "ESRC." At its broadest and least concrete, this argument underlines the didactic value of *The Wire* "as a conversation starter about crises of the human condition" (with all the troubling implications this phrase holds for an auto-utilitarian theory of didactics). At least one contribution to the ESRC conference feels it has to stress that *The Wire*, despite its utility for the classroom, "should not be regarded as a replacement for qualitative ethnographic research" (ibid.).

74 A point also suggested in Williams, "Ethnographic," although with an unqualified affirmation of the epistemological power of fiction. Williams lauds Simon's storytelling for reaching "beyond 'academic forms'" in order to achieve their highest ambitions: "it approaches what the ethnographer could only dream of: a multisited ethnographic imaginary that no longer needs to depend upon allusions to abstract ideas of the state, the economy, or capitalism to be understood in a more concrete, vivid, and accessible form. The vivid and concrete interlocking stories are what fiction affords, what ethnography aspires to, and what newspaper journalism can only rarely achieve" ("Ethnographic," 215).

75 Wilson and Chaddha, "Why We're Teaching 'The Wire' at Harvard."

76 See Wilson, *When Work Disappears*; also Gilens, *Why Americans Hate Welfare*.

77 Walter Benn Michaels's endorsement of the series follows similar insights; see "Going Boom."

78 Chaddha and Wilson, "Way," 188.

79 Warren, "Sociology and *The Wire*," 200.

80 Ibid. For Simon citing Wilson, see Carioli, "*The Wire*'s David Simon."

81 On Park and *The Wire*, see Lemann, "Charm City"; also quoted in Chaddha and Wilson, "Way," 166.

82 For HOPE VI, see Warren, "Response": a text that takes pains not to accuse Wilson personally and yet suggests repeatedly that sociologists bear some kind of responsibility for the political uses made of their research.

83 From the perspective of a Marxist explanatory system, research like Wilson's has played its part in neoliberal policies simply by downplaying class in favor of race and culture. In his initial response to Chaddha and Wilson, Warren writes: "The crucial point here is that Wilson's 'analytic perspective' is not just a window onto how the urban poor were dislocated during the late twentieth century. *Rather, Wilson's sociology was also part of that process of dislocation.* All that is in question here is whether or not the cynical appropriation of sociological ideas by real estate developers adequately explains how Wilson's ideas came to play the role they played. . . . It might seem curious that at a moment when capitalist interests were taking the gloves off in their fight against all other sectors of society the dominant sociological model of poverty became one that subordinated politics to neighborhood demographics. . . . This does not mean that social science scholars always knowingly or intentionally trim their sails to catch the prevailing winds of naked class interest (although there are plenty instances of this). But it does mean that any reflection on the prominence of academic models ought to include at least a brief glance at whose interests might be served should analysis become policy" ("Sociology," 205-6). On the logic of critical one-upmanship in American Studies, see Fluck, "The Humanities in the Age of Expressive Individualism and Cultural Radicalism."

84 Somewhat unnerved, Wilson writes in his final rejoinder to Warren: "it is clear that *The Wire* has become incidental to his

arguments" ("Response"). This is true, but Wilson and Chaddha in their original essay also treated the show as an occasion to showcase their field and their policy allegiances.

85 Warren, "Sociology," 201; Chaddha and Wilson, "*The Wire's* Impact," 228.

86 Chaddha and Wilson, "Impact," 228.

87 "ESRC."

88 The ESRC conference describes the television series as a "popular culture laboratory," where "ethnographic research on the city" is "translated" into fiction. Thus, *The Wire's* representation of Baltimore's educational system is described as "one of the ideal frames where the fictional side of the show turns into reality" ("ESRC").

89 See Alff, "Yesterday's Tomorrow Today," reading *The Wire* as "a televisual annotation of regional history" (26).

90 See the definition of *The Wire* as an "obsodrama": a documentary that has been fictionalized to remove legal constraints ("ESRC"). Compare also Clandfield about the show's "constructive use of fictional license" and its "legitimate tactical response to the misrepresentation of inner cities" ("We," 44).

91 "ESRC."

92 See Gibb and Sabin, "Who Loves Ya, David Simon?" Even the representation of sex seems driven by an attempt at inverting stereotypes: Sexual relations between white characters in *The Wire* are marked by a passionate loss of control, whereas sexual relations between black characters are largely depicted as caring and sensuous affairs. (I am indebted to Markus Engelhardt for this observation.)

93 Cormier, "Bringing Omar Back to Life."

94 Williams, "The Lost Boys of Baltimore," 58. Williams continues: "[*The Wire*] evokes at times the imagery of black homo-thug gay porn websites." Gangster hunks and dashing officers "in their heightened availability and

vulnerability [constitute] one of the great unavowed pleasures of *The Wire*. What is one person's urban nightmare is another man's fantasy" (59).

95 McNeil, "White Negroes and *The Wire*."

96 Weaver, "Baltimore before *The Wire*," 16-18. For "documentary fallacy," see Marshall and Potter, "I am the American Dream," 9.

97 Franklin, "Common Ground."

98 Lander, *Stuff White People Like*, 108-10.

99 "We, *The Wire* Discussion Group at the University of Leeds" takes collective hold of the drama of marginalization, declaring that "the series also came to symbolise our own problematic relationship with an academic institution in which we all play, at best, marginal roles" ("ESRC").

100 Marshall and Potter, "I am," 13.

101 Kelly, "Casting *The Wire*." On the nexus of reality and the hardboiled life, see Chapter Three.

102 Marshall and Potter, "I am," 12. *The New York Times* called the wedding "a street version of Cinderella and Prince Charming" (Urbina, "From Two Broken Lives"). Simon himself pitched the story to the *Times*, insisting that there would be not only an article but also a "Vows" piece (Talbot, "Stealing").

103 Kelly, "Casting." See also Marshall and Potter, "I am," 10.

104 Kinder, "Re-Writing Baltimore," 54. See also Kelly, "Casting."

105 Compare Kelleter, "Serienhelden sehen dich an," 73; similarly Sharma, "All the pieces matter." Jagoda sees the show "avoiding technological determinism" ("Wired," 191) but this seems to be a euphemism for *The Wire*'s silence about (its own) technological agency.

106 Venkatesh, "What Do Real Thugs Think of *The Wire*? Part Seven."

107 Venkatesh, *Gang Leader for a Day*, "What Do Real Thugs [Part

One]," "What Do Real Thugs, Part Three."

108 Bowden, "Angriest."

109 Especially Ethridge, "Baltimore." See also Salam who holds that the series' fatalism "transcends ideology: it strengthens the hand of paternalists of the left and determinists of the right. In that regard, the show is frankly destructive" ("The Bleakness of *The Wire*"). Johnson-Lewis, oddly to me, sees a contradiction between *The Wire*'s interest in institutional structures (its fatalism) and the supposedly detrimental effects of extended serial storytelling on activist empathy: "it wallows far too long in the decay and dejection of contemporary urban life" ("The More Things Change, The More They Stay the Same").

110 See Salam: "I'm struck by how many of my friends believe they have more refined moral sensibilities because they watch and swear by *The Wire*, as though it gives them a richer appreciation of the *real* struggles of inner-city life, despite the fact that they are exactly as insulated as they were before" ("Bleakness"). Similarly, Johnson-Lewis argues that the show "leave[s] the viewer to feel secure in his or her moral superiority for watching the gritty realism of *The Wire*" ("More").

111 For "irredeemable," see Johnson-Lewis, "More."

112 Dreier and Atlas, "Bush-Era Fable about America's Urban Poor," 332. The authors see *The Wire* as "similar to much of American sociology" in this regard, "which, despite its reform impulse, is better at describing the various forms of inequality and injustice in society than at identifying the political opportunities that make mobilization and reform possible" (331).

113 Ethridge, "Baltimore," 163-64.

114 Bowden, "Angriest"; Dreier and Atlas, "Bush-Era," 332-33.

115 The record may be less impressive for female characters. For Omar as "a kind of *agent provocateur*," see LeBesco,

"Gots to Get Got," 217. Chaddha and Wilson make a similar claim concerning *The Wire*'s (supposed) eschewal of individual heroism or failure: "Americans remain strongly disposed to the idea that individuals are largely responsible for their own economic situations. . . . *The Wire* effectively undermines such views by showing how the decisions people make are profoundly influenced by their environment or social circumstances" ("Way Down," 165). However, this insight does not lead Chaddha and Wilson to investigate the series as a cultural agent in its own right. Seeing *The Wire* as a faithful illustration of their own systemic approach to urban inequality, they also ignore activities of the series that would point in an altogether different direction (e.g., its investment in existentialist notions of heroism).

116 Lanahan, "Secrets," 29.
117 Burns et al., "*The Wire*'s War on the Drug War."
118 McMillan, "Dramatizing Individuation."
119 Ibid.
120 McMillan, "Heroism, Institutions, and the Police Procedural," 53.
121 Fuggle, "Short-Circuiting the Power Grid"; McMillan, "Dramatizing"; McMillan, "Heroism," 54; Herring, "There's never been a paper bag for drugs."
122 McMillan, "Heroism," 51.
123 "[It] doesn't simply reproduce or 'comment' upon social reality, but sets out instead to unravel the twisted fabric of social assemblages" (McMillan, "Dramatizing").
124 Perhaps Linda Williams's tribute to the (social) force of (melodramatic) fiction in *The Wire* comes close, praising how the series modernizes sentimental storytelling in order to capture complex realities that lie outside the representational scope of journalistic and academic writing ("Ethnographic").

125 McMillan, "Dramatizing." Also see Herring about *The Wire*'s potential "to resist discipline" ("There"); compare also Sharma, "All."

126 Schaub, "Big Brother Is Not Watching You," 126. Schaub writes: "The fact that *The Wire* uses the banner of 'fiction' to tell stories premised on reality should hardly come as a surprise in an era when the banner of 'reality' is so often used to market shows with an obviously fictitious premise" (ibid. 130). Schaub does not address *The Wire*'s own narcissistic promptings within and without its narrative. Instead, he accepts Season Five's characterization of the series as media-critical "watchdog for democracy" (ibid.).

127 Compare Latour about "the dramatic lesson" of "the transatlantic destiny of Michel Foucault": "No one was more precise in his analytical decomposition of the tiny ingredients from which power is made and no one was more critical of social explanations [i.e., critical of invoking "an invisible, unmovable, and homogeneous world of power," F.K.]. And yet, as soon as Foucault was translated, he was immediately turned into the one who had 'revealed' power relations *behind* every innocuous activity: madness, natural history, sex, administration, etc. This proves again with what energy the notion of social explanation should be fought: even the genius of Foucault could not prevent such a total inversion" (*Reassembling*, 86).

128 See Rowe and Collins, "Power *Wire*": "our study found that *The Wire* was not entirely successful at avoiding clichés and stereotypes that are entrenched in most procedural crime dramas." At the same time, the study describes Foucault's concept of governmentality as "one of the most useful . . . explanations of power" because it supposedly demonstrates "that Western liberal democracies have systematically found ways to assert control over virtually every aspect of life" (182).

129 Taylor, "Investigating the Use of a Neoliberal Institutional Apparatus."

130 Brooks, "The Narrative Production of 'Real Police'," 73. The following quote ibid. 64-66.

131 Nannicelli, "All," 190.

132 See Nannicelli declaring that *The Wire* is less conventional than the cinematic "network narratives" analyzed by David Bordwell and Kristen Thompson (ibid. 195).

133 Kinder, "Re-Writing," 54.

134 Gibb and Sabin, "Who." For *Dragnet*, see Mittell, "All," 434, *Television*, 181, and especially *Genre and Television*, 121-52.

135 Mittell, "All," 429, 434, 431. Quotations in the following paragraph ibid. 433, 432, 435.

136 In addition to the contributions mentioned in this chapter and some more in the following chapter, there are, as far as I can see, only few attempts to discuss *The Wire* in such terms, mostly focused on generic configurations. Amanda Klein examines the show's adherence to and deviation from conventions of melodrama and sentimentality ("The Dickensian Aspect"). Similarly, Linda Williams taught the series at UC Berkeley with regard to its melodramatic aspects (Bennett, "This Will Be on the Midterm") and has a book forthcoming on this theme. Jagoda writes: "*The Wire* is less a map of a social totality than a means of modulating the relations between narrative forms within a dynamic and changing social sphere" ("Wired," 199).

137 "More likely" does not mean "generally predisposed." Celebratory readings prevail in non-American settings as well, including my own academic culture in Germany.

138 "ESRC." Bramall and Pitcher's paper has in the meantime been published as "Policing the Crisis, or, Why We Love *The Wire*."

139 Alvarez, *Truth*, 37-41.

140 Mosley, "1926: It is awfully easy to be hardboiled," 598.

141 Alvarez, *Truth*, 126.

142 Hornby, "David."

143 "Conversation with David Simon."

144 Scott, "Who."

145 Mosley, "1926," 598. Mosley's own affirmation of the hardboiled ethos depends on his understanding of the blues as a black expression of perseverance in the face of adversity, now open to all Americans (see Stein, "Walter Mosley's *RL's Dream*").

146 Hornby, "David." The quotation is from a different interview: O'Rourke, "Behind."

147 Memorably described in Fiedler, *Love and Death in the American Novel*.

148 Klein, "Dickensian," 178. Klein goes on to argue that *The Wire* also "denies or subverts several key melodramatic pleasures," such as "the catharsis of tears, narrative closure, moral legibility, individualistic solutions to social problems, and nostalgia" (179) – all actually cherished by many viewers as its most satisfying provisions, sometimes by Simon himself: "I am very cynical about institutions. ... I am not cynical when it comes to individuals and people" (Moyers, "Simon"). Williams, too, identifies a modern surplus in Simon's melodrama: "The serial melodrama of *The Wire* differs from ordinary melodrama in its focus on the villainy of institutions as much as personal villains" ("Ethnographic," 219). Some would argue that already *Uncle Tom's Cabin* presented its personal villains as victims, in their turn, of the "peculiar institution." For nostalgia in *The Wire*, see this chapter's next section.

149 Is it necessary to stress that this flattening out of the culture's basic political distinctions does not claim to have uncovered a common determinator that cancels their real differences? It probably is. The point is to trace active habits that make such differences possible in the first place.

150 Mittell, "All," 431. If "real" is a dominant key term in American responses to *The Wire*, "human" is another.

151 Alvarez, "The Archdiocese of Narrative," 52.

152 Mittell, *Television*, 289.

153 Warhol, *Having a Good Cry*.

154 For the media dimensions of James Madison's oxymoronic concept of an "extended republic," see Kelleter, *Amerikanische Aufklärung*, 474-546.

155 Mittell, *Television*, 318, 323. Simon's HBO series *Treme*, about post-Katrina New Orleans, is another project that seeks to counteract the effects of media inattention. The show's casting policies, on-location production, and authenticating paratexts parallel strategies employed by *The Wire*, but this time with the explicit intention of boosting (an alternative type of) tourism to the area – a motivation that tries to take care of activist concerns but raises anxieties about insider knowledge and "complicity" even greater than in *The Wire*.

156 As an example of the first reading, see Williams, "Ethnographic," 214. The show itself describes this type of social vision as looking with "soft eyes" (the title of episode 4.2).

157 Simon in Alvarez, *Truth*, 123.

158 Moyers, "Simon."

159 On FDR's Fireside Chats and their importance for American popular seriality, see Kelleter, "Trust and Sprawl."

160 Toscano and Kinkle, "Baltimore as World and Representation." Again it is interesting that British scholars have drawn this map. In the United States, more importance is accorded to classifying the series in terms of current self-descriptions of American politics (as torn between "liberalism" and "conservatism"), with *The Wire* sometimes framed as a far-left or "Marxist" text in this field.

161 Compare Kraniauskas, another London-based scholar: "Work is a structuring ideologeme of the series"

("Elasticity," 26).

162 See Shales, offering what sounds like a textbook definition of existential heroism: "[The characters] suffer more defeats than they score victories, but just hanging in there is victory in itself" ("In Season 4").

163 Simon, "Introduction," 31.

164 Simon, "Letter," 34.

165 Simon, "Introduction," 22.

166 Moore, "In the Life of 'The Wire'," 23.

167 Sheehan and Sweeney, "*The Wire* and the World."

168 Gardner, "The Birth of the Open-Ended Serial."

169 Gardner, ibid., quoting Crawford. These considerations are compatible with Winfried Fluck's remarkable Tocquevillian project of reading American cultural history through the lens of "recognition" (see, for example, "Fiction and the Struggle for Recognition").

170 On the power of naturalistic styles to make viewers "lose" themselves, see Mittell, *Television*, 162. On the power of fiction to make readers find themselves, see Fluck, "Why We Need Fiction."

171 Rivers, "Obama in the Age of 'The Wire.'"

172 Mittell, *Television*, 289. For an empirical investigation into the reality of the *CSI* effect, see Tyler, "Viewing *CSI*." Tyler concludes that the notion of targeted or unified media influence on legal practice (as it dominates the print media's invocation of a *CSI* effect) is misguided. Watching *CSI* and other procedural or courtroom dramas produces a range of social effects, in the plural, many of which contradict the impact specifically ascribed to *CSI*.

173 Manjoo, *True Enough*.

174 Hornby, "David."

175 Alvarez, *Truth*, 414.

176 Weaver, "Baltimore," 20.

177 Alvarez, *Truth*, 232.

178 Schaub, "Big," 130.
179 Alvarez, *Truth*, 233.
180 Bowden, "Angriest."

Works Cited

Aiello, Ryan. "*The Wire*: Politics, Postmodernism and the Rebirth of American Naturalism." MA thesis. California State University, Cico, 2010.

Alvarez, Rafael, ed. 2009. *The Wire: Truth Be Told.* Edinburgh: Canongate, 2009.

— "The Archdiocese of Narrative." *Third Person: Authoring and Exploring Vast Narratives.* Ed. Pat Harrigan and Noah Wardrip-Fruin. Cambridge: MIT, 2009. 49-57.

Anderson, Angela. "No Such Thing as Good and Evil: *The Wire* and the Humanization of the Object of Risk in the Age of Biopolitics." *darkmatter* 4 (2009). Web. 7 Oct. 2010. <http://www.darkmatter101.org/site/2009/05/29/no-such-thing-as-good-and-evil-thewire-and-the-humanization-of-the-object-of-risk-in-the-age-of-biopolitics/>

Anderson, Elijah. *A Place on the Corner.* Chicago: U Chicago P, 1978.

— *Streetwise: Race, Class, and Change in an Urban Community.* Chicago: U Chicago P, 1990.

— *Code of the Street: Decency, Violence, and the Moral Life of the Inner City.* New York: Norton, 2003.

Beliveau, Ralph, and Laura Bolf-Beliveau. "Posing Problems and Picking Fights: Critical Pedagogy and the Corner Boys." *The Wire: Urban Decay and American Television.* Ed. Tiffany Potter and C. W. Marshall. New York: Continuum, 2009. 91-103.

Bennett, Drake. "This Will Be on Midterm. You Feel Me?" *Slate* (24 March 2010). Web. 8 Jul. 2010. http://www.slate.com/id/2245788/

Bieger, Laura. "'It's All in the Game': David Simons *The Wire* als naturalistische Krisenerzählung." *American Dream? Eine Weltmacht in der Krise.* Ed. Andreas Etges and Winfried Fluck. München: Campus, 2011. 215-240.

Blumer, Herbert. *Symbolic Interactionism: Perspective and Method.* Englewood Cliffs: Prentice-Hall, 1969.

Blundell, Boyd. "Social Justice and the Wire." Department of Religious Studies, Loyola University, First-year seminar syllabus (2009). Web. 8 Jul. 2010. http://img.slate.com/media/8/WireSyllabus.pdf

Bowden, Mark. "The Angriest Man in Television." *The Atlantic* (January 2008). Web. 7 Oct. 2010. http://www.theatlantic.com/magazine/archive/2008/01/the-angriest-man-in-television/6581

Bramall, Rebecca, and Ben Pitcher. "Policing the Crisis, or, *Why We Love The Wire.*" *International Journal of Cultural Studies* 16 (2013): 85-98.

Brooks, Ryan. "The Narrative Production of 'Real Police'." *The Wire: Urban Decay and American Television.* Ed. Tiffany Potter and C. W. Marshall. New York: Continuum, 2009. 64-77.

Burkeman, Olivier. "Arrogant? Moi?" *The Guardian* (28 March 2009). Web. 18 Oct. 2010. http://www.guardian.co.uk/media/2009/mar/28/david-simon-the-wire-interview

Burns, Ed, Dennis Lehane, George Pelecanos, Richard Price, and David Simon. "*The Wire*'s War on the Drug War." *Time Magazine* (5 March 2008). Web. 7 Oct. 2010. http://www.time.com/time/nation/article/0,8599,1719872,00.html

Carioli, Carly. "*The Wire*'s David Simon at Harvard." *The Pholg* (8 April 2008). Web. 26 Dec. 2013. thephoenix.com/BLOGS/phlog/archive/2008/04/08/video-the-wire-s-david-simon-at-harvard.aspx

Chaddha, Anmol, and William Julius Wilson. "'Way Down in the Hole': Systemic Urban Inequality and The Wire." *Critical Inquiry* 38 (2011): 164-188.

— "*Critical Response IV: The Wire's* Impact: A Rejoinder." *Critical Inquiry* 38 (2011): 227-233.

Clandfield, Peter. "'We ain't got no yard': Crime, Development, and Urban Environment." *The Wire: Urban Decay and American*

Television. Ed. Tiffany Potter and C. W. Marshall. New York: Continuum, 2009. 37-49.

"Conversation with David Simon at Eugene Lang College, The New School for Liberal Arts." *The Wire: The Complete Third Season*. HBO, 2007. DVD.

Cormier, Harvey. "Bringing Omar Back to Life." *Journal of Speculative Philosophy* 22.3 (2008): 205-213.

Dignan, Andrew. "*The Wire* and the Art of the Credit Sequence." *Slant* (22 September 2006). Web. 19 Oct. 2010. http://www.slantmagazine.com/house/2006/09/the-wire-and-the-art-of-the-credit-sequence

Dreier, Peter, and John Atlas. "Bush-Era Fable about America's Urban Poor?" *City & Community* 8.3 (2009): 329-340. Reprint in *The Wire: Race, Class, and Genre*. Ann Arbor: U Michigan P, 2012. 130-146.

Edgerton, Gary R., and Jeffrey P. Jones, eds. 2008. *The Essential HBO Reader*. Lexington: UP Kentucky, 2008.

"ESRC Centre for Research on Socio-Cultural Change Conference: The Wire as Social Science Fiction? 26-27 November 2009, Leeds Town Hall. Conference Outline." ESRC Centre for Research on Socio-Cultural Change, n.d. Web. 15 Oct. 2010. http://www.cresc.ac.uk/events/Wireconference.html; www.cresc.ac.uk/events/wire_programme.html

Ethridge, Blake D. "Baltimore on *The Wire*: The Tragic Moralism of David Simon." *It's Not TV: Watching HBO in the Post-Television Era*. Ed. Marc Leverette, Brian L. Ott, and Cara Louise Buckley. New York: Routledge, 2008. 152-164.

Feuer, Jane, Paul Kerr, and Tise Vahimagi, eds. *MTM – "Quality Television"*. London: BFI, 1984.

Fiedler, Leslie. *Love and Death in the American Novel*. 1960. New York: Dell, 1969.

Fluck, Winfried. "The Humanities in the Age of Expressive Individualism and Cultural Radicalism." 1998. *Romance with America?* Ed. Laura Bieger and Johannes Voelz. Heidelberg:

Winter, 2009. 49-68.

— "Why We Need Fiction: Reception Aesthetics, Literary Anthropology, *Funktionsgeschichte*." 2002. *Romance with America?* Ed. Laura Bieger and Johannes Voelz. Heidelberg: Winter, 2009. 365-384.

— "Fiction and the Struggle for Recognition." *Tocqueville's Legacy: Towards a Cultural History of Recognition in American Studies.* Ed. Winfried Fluck. Special Issue of *Amerikastudien/American Studies* 57 (2012): 689-709.

Franklin, Judd. "Common Ground: The Political Economy of *The Wire.*" *darkmatter* 4 (2009). Web. 15 Oct. 2010. http://www.darkmatter101.org/site/2009/05/29/common-ground-thepo litical-economy-of-the-wire/

Fuggle, Sophie. "Short Circuiting the Power Grid: *The Wire* as Critique of Institutional Power." *darkmatter* 4 (2009). Web. 7 Oct. 2010. http://www.darkmatter101.org/site/2009/05/29/sh ortcircuiting-the-power-grid-the-wire-as-critique-of-institu tional-power/

Gardner, Jared. "The Birth of the Open-Ended Serial and The Future of Storytelling." Lecture at Georg-August-Universität Göttingen, 17 May 2011.

Gibb, Jane, and Roger Sabin. "Who Loves Ya, David Simon?" *darkmatter* 4 (2009). Web. 7 Oct. 2010. http://www.dark matter101.org/site/2009/05/29/who-loves-ya-david-simon

Gilens, Martin. *Why Americans Hate Welfare: Race, Media, and the Politics of Antipoverty Policy.* Chicago: U Chicago P, 1999.

Harrigan, Pat, and Noah Wardrip-Fruin, eds. *Third Person: Authoring and Exploring Vast Narratives.* Boston: MIT, 2009.

Havrilesky, Heather. "David Simon on Cutting 'The Wire'." *Salon* (10 March 2008). Web. 24 Jun. 2010. http://www.salon .com/entertainment/tv/feature/2008/03/10/simon

Hayward, Jennifer. *Consuming Pleasures: Active Audiences and Serial Fictions from Dickens to Soap Opera.* 1997. Lexington: UP Kentucky, 2008.

Herring, William Rodney. "'There's never been a paper bag for drugs. Until now.' Or, What Is 'Real Police Work'?" William Rodney Herring (18 February 2008). Web. 24 Jun. 2010. http://locus.cwrl.utexas.edu/herring/node/111

Hornby, Nick. "David Simon: Personal Interview." *Believer* (August 2008). Web. 24 Jun. 2010. http://www.believermag.com/issues/200708/?read=interview_simon

Jahn-Sudmann, Andreas. "Serienzeit und serielle Zeitlichkeit." Rev. of *'Previously On ... ' Zur Ästhetik der Zeitlichkeit neuerer TV-Serien*, by Arno Meteling, Isabell Otto und Gabriele Schabacher." *Zeitschrift für Medienwissenschaft* (March 2011). Web. 20 May 2011. http://www.zfmedienwissenschaft.de/index.php?TID=54

— and Frank Kelleter. "Die Dynamik serieller Überbietung: Amerikanische Fernsehserien und das Konzept des Quality-TV." *Populäre Serialität: Narration-Evolution-Distinktion. Zum seriellen Erzählen seit dem 19. Jahrhundert*. Ed. Frank Kelleter. Bielefeld: transcript, 2012. 205-224.

— and Alexander Starre. "Die Experimente des 'Quality TV': Innovation und Metamedialität in neueren amerikanischen Serien." *Transnationale Serienkultur: Theorie, Ästhetik, Narration und Rezeption neuer Fernsehserien*. Ed. Susanne Eichner et al. Wiesbaden: VS, 2013. 103-119.

Jagoda, Patrick. "Critical Response I: Wired." *Critical Inquiry* 38 (2011): 189-199.

Johnson-Lewis, Erika. "The More Things Change, the More They Stay the Same: Serial Narrative on *The Wire*." *darkmatter* 4 (2009). Web. 7 Oct. 2010. http://www.darkmatter101.org/site/2009/05/29/the-more-things-change-the-more-theystay-the-same-serial-narrative-on-the-wire/

Kelleter, Frank. *Amerikanische Aufklärung: Sprachen der Rationalität im Zeitalter der Revolution*. Paderborn: Schöningh, 2002.

— "Transnationalism: The American Challenge." *Review of*

International American Studies 2.3 (2007): 29-33.

— "Populärkultur und Kanonisierung: Wie(so) erinnern wir uns an Tony Soprano?" *Wertung und Kanon*. Ed. Matthias Freise and Claudia Stockinger. Heidelberg: Winter, 2010. 55-76.

— "Serienhelden sehen dich an." *Psychologie Heute* 38.4 (2011): 70-75.

— "Populäre Serialität: Eine Einführung." *Populäre Serialität: Narration-Evolution-Distinktion. Zum seriellen Erzählen seit dem 19. Jahrhundert*. Ed. Frank Kelleter. Bielefeld: transcript, 2012. 11-46.

— "'Toto, I think we're in Oz again (and again and again)': Remakes and Popular Seriality." *Film Remakes, Adaptations and Fan Productions: Remake/Remodel*. Ed. Kathleen Loock and Constantine Verevis. Basingstoke: Palgrave Macmillan. 19-44.

— "*The Wire* and Its Readers." *The Wire: Race, Class, and Genre*. Ed. Liam Kennedy and Stephen Shapiro. Ann Arbor: U Michigan P, 2012. 33-70.

— "Trust and Sprawl: Seriality, Radio, and the First Fireside Chat." *Media Economies*. Ed. Marcel Hartwig, Evelyn Keitel, and Gunter Süß. Trier: wvt (forthcoming).

— "'Whatever Happened, Happened': Serial Character Constellation as Problem and Solution in *Lost*." *American Television Series*. [Working Title.] Ed. Heike Paul and Christoph Ernst. Bielefeld: transcript (forthcoming).

— ed. *Populäre Serialität: Narration-Evolution-Distinktion. Zum seriellen Erzählen seit dem 19. Jahrhundert*. Bielefeld: transcript, 2012.

— and Daniel Stein. "Autorisierungspraktiken seriellen Erzählens: Zur Gattungsentwicklung von Superhelden-comics." *Populäre Serialität: Narration-Evolution-Distinktion. Zum seriellen Erzählen seit dem 19. Jahrhundert*. Ed. Frank Kelleter. Bielefeld: transcript, 2012. 259-290.

Kelly, Lisa W. "Casting *The Wire*: Complicating Notions of

Performance, Authenticity, and 'Otherness'." *darkmatter* 4 (2009). Web. 7 Jun. 2010. http://www.darkmatter101 .org/site/2009/05/29/casting-the-wire-complicating-notionsof-performance-authenticity-and-otherness/

Kennedy, Liam, and Stephen Shapiro, eds. *"The Wire": Race, Class, and Genre.* Ann Arbor: U Michigan P, 2012.

Kinder, Marsha. "Re-Writing Baltimore: The Emotive Power of Systemics, Seriality, and the City." *Film Quarterly* 62.2 (2008): 50-57. Reprint in: *The Wire: Race, Class, and Genre.* Ed. Liam Kennedy and Stephen Shapiro. Ann Arbor: U Michigan P, 2012. 71-83.

King, Jim. "Exclusive David Simon Q & A: Personal Interview." *Borderline Productions* (16 August 2006). Web. 7 Jun. 2010. http://www.Borderline-productions.com/TheWire HBO/exclusive-1.html.

Klein, Amanda Ann. "'The Dickensian Aspect': Melodrama, Viewer Engagement, and the Socially Conscious Text." *The Wire: Urban Decay and American Television.* Ed. Tiffany Potter and C. W. Marshall. New York: Continuum, 2009. 177-189.

Kois, Adam, and Adam Sternbergh. "Debating the Legacy of 'The Wire': Did Season Five Tarnish the Show that Invented the Dickensian Aspect Ratio." *New York Magazine* (7 March 2008). Web. 20 Oct. 2010. http://www.nymag.com/daily/enter tainment/2008/03/debating_the_end_of_the_wire_t.html

Kraniauskas, John. "Elasticity of Demand: Reflections on *The Wire*." *Radical Philosophy* 154 (2009): 25-34. Reprint in: *The Wire: Race, Class, and Genre.* Ed. Liam Kennedy and Stephen Shapiro. Ann Arbor: U Michigan P, 2012. 170-192.

Lanahan, Lawrence. "Secrets of the City: What *The Wire* Reveals About Urban Journalism." *Columbia Journalism Review* (January/February 2008): 22-31.

Lander, Christian. *Stuff White People Like: The Definitive Guide to the Unique Taste of Millions.* New York: Random House, 2008.

Latour, Bruno. *Reassembling the Social: An Introduction to Actor-*

Network-Theory. Oxford: Oxford UP, 2005.

LeBesco, Kathleen. "'Gots to Get Got': Social Justice and Audience Response to Omar Little." *The Wire: Urban Decay and American Television*. Ed. Tiffany Potter and C. W. Marshall. New York: Continuum, 2009. 217-232.

Lemann, Nicholas. "Charm City, USA." *New York Review of Books* 57.14 (September 30-October 13, 2010): 49-51.

Leverette, Marc, Brian L. Ott, and Carla Lousie Buckley, eds. *It's Not TV: Watching HBO in the Post-Television Era*. New York: Routledge, 2008.

Lowry, Brian. "The Wire." *Variety* (7 September 2006). Web. 1 Jun. 2010. http://www.variety.com/awardcentral_review/VE11179 31487.html?nav=reviews07&categoryid=2352&cs=1&p=0

Luhmann, Niklas. *Die Gesellschaft der Gesellschaft*. 1997. Frankfurt: Suhrkamp, 1999.

Manjoo, Farhad. *True Enough: Learning to Live in a Post-Fact Society*. Hoboken: John Wiley, 2008.

Marcus, George E. *Ethnography through Thick and Thin*. Princeton: Princeton UP, 1998.

Marshall, Courtney and Tiffany Potter. "'I am the American Dream': Modern Urban Tragedy and the Borders of Fiction." *The Wire: Urban Decay and American Television*. Ed. Tiffany Potter and C. W. Marshall. New York: Continuum, 2009.1-14.

Martin, Brett. *Difficult Men. Behind the Scenes of a Creative Revolution: From* The Sopranos *and* The Wire *to* Mad Men *and* Breaking Bad. New York: Penguin, 2013.

Mayer, Ruth. *Serial Fu Manchu: The Chinese Supervillain and the Spread of Yellow Peril Ideology*. Philadelphia: Temple UP, 2013.

McMillan, Alasdair. "Dramatizing Individuation: Institutions, Assemblages, and The Wire." *Cinephile: The University of British Columbia's Film Journal* 4 (2008). Web. 10 Jun. 2010. http://cinephile.ca/archives/volume-4-post-genre/drama tizing-individuation-institutions-assemblages-and-the-wire

— "Heroism, Institutions, and the Police Procedural." *The*

Wire: Urban Decay and American Television. Ed. Tiffany Potter and C. W. Marshall. New York: Continuum, 2009. 50-63.

McNeil, Daniel. "White Negroes and *The Wire.*" *darkmatter* 4 (2009). Web. 7 Oct. 2010. http://www.darkmatter101.org/site/2009/05/29/white-negroes-and-the-wire/

Michaels, Walter Benn. "Going Boom." *Bookforum* (February/March 2009). Web. 7 Oct. 2010. <http:www.bookforum.com/inprint/015_05/3274>

Mittell, Jason. *Genre and Television: From Cop Shows to Cartoons in American Culture.* New York: Routledge, 2004.

— "Narrative Complexity and American Television." *The Velvet Light Trap* 58 (2006): 29-40.

— "All in the Game: *The Wire,* Serial Storytelling, and Procedural Logic." *Third Person: Authoring and Exploring Vast Narratives.* Ed. Pat Harrigan and Noah Wardip-Fruin. Boston: MIT, 429-438.

— "The Television Context for *The Wire.*" Watching The Wire (3 February 2009). Web. 15 Oct. 2010. http://blogs.middlebury.edu/thewire/context-television

— *Television and American Culture.* New York: Oxford UP, 2010.

Moore, Lorrie. "In the Life of 'The Wire.'" *The New York Review of Books* 57.15 (October 14-27, 2010): 23-25.

Mosley, Walter. "1926: 'It is awfully easy to be hard-boiled about everything in the daytime, but at night it is another thing.'" *A New Literary History of America.* Ed. Greil Marcus and Werner Sollors. Cambridge: Harvard UP, 2010. 598-602.

Moyers, Bill. "Simon on Fact and Fiction." *Bill Moyers Journal* (2008). Web. 7 Oct. 2010. http://www.pbs.org/moyers/journal/04172009/transcript1.html

Nannicelli, Ted. "It's All Connected: Televisual Narrative Complexity." *The Wire: Urban Decay and American Television.* Ed. Tiffany Potter and C.W. Marshall. New York: Continuum, 2009. 190-202.

Newcomb, Horace. "*Magnum, P.I.*: The Champagne of TV." *Channels of Communication* (May/June 1985): 23-26.

Newcomb, Horace, and Paul M. Hirsch. "Television as a Cultural Forum." 1976. *Television: The Critical View.* New York: Oxford UP, 1994. 503-515.

O'Rourke, Meghan. "Behind the Wire: David Simon and Where the Show Goes Next." *Slate* (1 December 2006). Web. 9 Jul. 2010. http://www.slate.com/id/2154694

Perren, Alisa. "I Don't Think We're in Hollywood Anymore: Television Series Go on Location." *Flow* (25 June 2008). Web. 9 Jul. 2010. http://flowtv.org/2008/06/i-don%E2%80%99t-think-we%E2%80%99re-in-hollywood-anymore-television-series-go-on-locationalisa-perren-georgia-state-university

Peterson, James Braxton. "Corner-Boy Masculinity: Intersections of Inner-City Manhood." *The Wire: Urban Decay and American Television.* Ed. Tiffany Potter and C. W. Marshall. New York: Continuum, 2009. 107-121.

Potter, Tiffany, and C. W. Marshall, eds. *The Wire: Urban Decay and American Television.* New York: Continuum, 2009.

Read, Jason. "Stringer Bell's Lament: Violence and Legitimacy in Contemporary Capitalism." *The Wire: Urban Decay and American Television.* Ed. Tiffany Potter and C. W. Marshall. New York: Continuum, 2009. 122-134.

Rivers, Eugene F. "Obama in the Age of 'The Wire.'" Fall 2010 Study Group. Web. 12 Oct. 2010. http://www.iop.harvard.edu/Programs/Fellows-Study-Groups/Fall-2010-Study-Groups/Obama-in-the-Age-of-%22The-Wire%22

Rowe, Dan, and Marti Cecilia Collins. "Power Wire: Understanding the Depiction of Power in TV Drama." *Journal of the Institute of Justice & International Studies* 9 (2009): 182-192.

Ryan, Maureen. "David Simon Talks about His Career in Journalism and the Final Chapter of 'The Wire'." *Chicago Tribune* (10 January 2008). Web. 18. Oct. 2010. http://features-blogs.chicagotribune.com/entertainment_tv/2008/01/davidsimontal.html

Salam, Reihan. "The Bleakness of *The Wire*." *The American Scene* (1 January 2008). Web. 20 Oct. 2010. <http://theamerican-scene.com/2008/01/01/the-bleakness-of-the-wire>

Schaub, Joseph Christopher. "*The Wire*: Big Brother Is Not Watching You in Bodymore, Murdaland." *Journal of Popular Film and Television* 38.3 (2010): 122-132.

Scott, Janny. "Who Gets to Tell a Black Story?" *New York Times* (11 June 2000). Web. 7 Oct. 2010. http://www.nytimes.com/library/national/race/061100scott-corner.html

Shales, Tom. "In Season 4 of 'The Wire,' Cable That Can't Be Touched." *Washington Post* (11 September 2006). Web. 1 Jun. 2010. http://www.washingtonpost.com/wpdyn/content/article/2006/09/10/AR2006091001162.html

Sharma, Ash. "'All the pieces matter': Introductory Notes on *The Wire*." *darkmatter* 4 (2009). Web. 7 Oct. 2010. http://www.darkmatter101.org/site/2009/05/29/editorial-all-thepieces-matter-introductory-notes-on-the-wire/

Sheehan, Helena, and Sheamus Sweeney. "*The Wire* and the World: Narrative and Metanarrative." *Jump Cut* 51 (2009). Web. 10 Jun. 2010. http://doras.dcu.ie/2459/1/jump-cut-doras.pdf

Sidhu, Dawinder S. "Wartime America and *The Wire*: A Response to Posner's Post-9/11 Constitutional Framework." *George Mason University Civil Rights Law Journal* 20.1 (2009). Web. 28 Aug. 2010. http://papers.ssrn.com/sol3/papers.cfm?abstract_id=1414006#%23

Simon, David. "Letter to HBO." 2001. *The Wire: Truth Be Told*. Ed. Rafael Alvarez. Edinburgh: Canongate, 2009. 32-36.

— "Introduction." *The Wire: Truth Be Told*. Ed. Rafael Alvarez. Edinburgh: Canongate, 2009. 1-31.

— "I meant this, not that." *The Audacity of Despair* (16 April 2012). Web. 9 Sep. 2013. http://davidsimon.com/i-meant-this/

Sodano, Todd. "Critic-Adored, Award-Ignored: Roots and

Consequences of Emmy Gone Wire-less." Paper presented at the annual meeting of the Association for Education in Journalism and Mass Communication, The Denver Sheraton, Denver, CO (4 August 2010). Web. 7 Oct. 2010. http://www.allacademic.com/meta/p434719_index.html

Stein, Daniel. "Walter Mosley's *RL's Dream* and the Creation of a Bluetopian Community." *Finding a Way Home: A Critical Assessment of Walter Mosley's Fiction*. Ed. Derek C. Maus and Owen E. Brady. Jackson: U Mississippi P, 2008. 3-17.

Sternbergh, Adam. "Sternbergh on 'The Wire' Finale: The Anti-'Sopranos'." *New York Magazine* (10 March 2008). Web. 19 Aug. 2010. http://nymag.com/daily/entertainment/2008/03/sternbergh_on_the_wire_finale.html

Suderman, Peter. "Tension City." *National Review* (21 April 2008): 59-60.

Talbot, Margaret. "Stealing Life: The Crusader behind 'The Wire'." *The New Yorker* (22 October 2007). Web. 9 Jul. 2010. http://www.www.newyorker.com/reporting/2007/10/22/071022fa_fact_talbot

Taylor, Sara. "*The Wire*: Investigating the Use of a Neoliberal Institutional Apparatus and a 'New Humanist' Philosophical Apparatus." *darkmatter* 4 (2009). Web. 7 Oct. 2010. http://www.darkmatter101.org/site/2009/05/29/the-wire-investigating-the-use-of-aneoliberal-institutional-apparatus-and-a-new-humanist-philosophical-apparatus/

Thompson, Robert J. *Television's Second Golden Age*. Syracuse: Syracuse UP, 1997.

Toscano, Alberto, and Jeff Kinkle. "Baltimore as World and Representation: Cognitive Mapping and Capitalism in *The Wire*." *Dossier* (8 April 2009). Web. 15 Oct. 2010. http://dossier-journal.com/read/theory/baltimore-as-world-and-representation-cognitivemapping-and-capitalism-in-the-wire/

Tucker, Ken. "High 'Wire': The End of a Masterpiece." *Entertainment Weekly* (14 March 2008). Web. 15 Oct. 2010.

http://www.ew.com/ew/article/0,,20184005,00.html

Tyler, Tom R. "Viewing *CSI* and the Threshold of Guilt: Managing Truth and Justice in Reality and Fiction." *The Yale Law Journal* 115 (2006): 1050-1085.

Tyree, J. M. "The Wire: The Complete Fourth Season." *Film Quarterly* 61.3 (2008): 32-39.

Urbina, Ian. "From Two Broken Lives to One Beginning." *New York Times* (9 August 2007). Web. 30 Sep. 2010. http://www.nytimes.com/2007/08/09/us/09baltimore.html?pagewanted=all

Venkatesh, Sudhir. *Gang Leader for a Day: A Rogue Sociologist Takes to the Streets.* New York: Penguin, 2008.

— "What Do Real Thugs Think of *The Wire*?" *Freakonomics* (9 January 2008). Web. 20 Oct. 2010. http://freakonomics.blogs.nytimes.com/2008/01/09/what-do-real-thugsthink-of-thewire/

— "What Do Real Thugs Think of *The Wire*? Part Three." *Freakonomics* (25 January 2008). Web. 20 Oct. 2010. http://freakonomics.blogs.nytimes.com/2008/01/25/what-do-real-thugs-think-of-thewire/

— "What Do Real Thugs Think of The Wire? Part Seven." *Freakonomics* (22 February 2008). Web. 20 Oct. 2010. http://freakonomics.blogs.nytimes.com/2008/02/22/what-do-real-thugs-think-of-thewire/

Warhol, Robyn. *Having a Good Cry: Effeminate Feelings and Popular Forms.* Columbus: Ohio State UP, 2003.

Warren, Kenneth W. "*Critical Response II:* Sociology and *The Wire.*" *Critical Inquiry* 38 (2011): 200-207.

— "Response." *The Wire: Continuing the Debate.* Critical Inquiry Online Features (29 November 2011). Web. 4 Oct. 2013. http://criticalinquiry.uchicago.edu/warrens_response/

Weaver, Afaa M. "Baltimore before *The Wire.*" *The Wire: Urban Decay and American Television.* Ed. Tiffany Potter and C. W. Marshall. New York: Continuum, 2009. 15-20.

Weisberg, Jacob. "The Wire on Fire: Analyzing the Best Show on

Television." *Slate* (13 September 2006). Web. 19 Aug. 2010. http://www.slate.com/id/2149566

Williams, James S. "The Lost Boys of Baltimore: Beauty and Desire in the Hood." *Film Quarterly* 62.2 (2008): 58-63.

Williams, Linda. *"Critical Response III:* Ethnographic Imaginary: The Genesis and Genius of *The Wire." Critical Inquiry* 38 (2011): 208-226.

Williams, Raymond. *Television: Technology and Cultural Form.* London: Fontana, 1974.

Wilson, William J. *When Work Disappears: The World of the New Urban Poor.* New York: Knopf, 1996.

— "Response." *The Wire: Continuing the Debate.* Critical Inquiry Online Features (29 November 2011). Web. 4 Oct. 2013. http://criticalinquiry.uchicago.edu/wilsons_response/

— and Anmol Chaddha. "Why We're Teaching 'The Wire' at Harvard." *Washington Post* (12 September 2010). Web. 12 Oct. 2010. http://www.hks.harvard.edu/newsevents/news/commentary/teaching-the-wire-at-harvard

Wolfe, Tom. "The New Journalism." 1973. *The New Journalism.* Ed. Tom Wolfe and E. W. Johnson. London: Picador, 1996.

Zborowski, James. "The Rhetoric of *The Wire." Movie: A Journal of Film Criticism* 1 (2010): 1-6. Web. 20 May 2011. http://www2.warwick.ac.uk/fac/arts/film/movie/contents/rhetoric_of_the_wire.pdf

Contemporary culture has eliminated both the concept of the
public and the figure of the intellectual. Former public spaces –
both physical and cultural – are now either derelict or colonized
by advertising. A cretinous anti-intellectualism presides,
cheerled by expensively educated hacks in the pay of
multinational corporations who reassure their bored readers
that there is no need to rouse themselves from their interpassive
stupor. The informal censorship internalized and propagated by
the cultural workers of late capitalism generates a banal
conformity that the propaganda chiefs of Stalinism could only
ever have dreamt of imposing. Zer0 Books knows that another
kind of discourse – intellectual without being academic, popular
without being populist – is not only possible: it is already
flourishing, in the regions beyond the striplit malls of so-called
mass media and the neurotically bureaucratic halls of the
academy. Zer0 is committed to the idea of publishing as a
making public of the intellectual. It is convinced that in
the unthinking, blandly consensual culture in which we live,
critical and engaged theoretical reflection is more important
than ever before.